KEY CONCEPTS IN VICTORIAN STUDIES

T0398809

Key Concepts in Literature

Published titles
Key Concepts in Literary Theory, 3rd edition
Julian Wolfreys, Ruth Robbins and Kenneth Womack

Key Concepts in Contemporary Popular Fiction
Bernice M. Murphy

Key Concepts in the Gothic
William Hughes

Key Concepts in Victorian Studies
William Hughes

www.edinburghuniversitypress.com/series/KCL

Key Concepts in Victorian Studies

William Hughes

EDINBURGH
University Press

Edinburgh University Press is one of the leading university presses in the UK. We publish academic books and journals in our selected subject areas across the humanities and social sciences, combining cutting-edge scholarship with high editorial and production values to produce academic works of lasting importance. For more information visit our website: edinburghuniversitypress.com

Edinburgh University Press Ltd
The Tun – Holyrood Road
12(2f) Jackson's Entry
Edinburgh EH8 8PJ

Typeset in 10/12 Adobe Sabon by
IDSUK (DataConnection) Ltd

A CIP record for this book is available from the British Library

ISBN 978 1 4744 9986 6 (hardback)
ISBN 978 1 4744 9987 3 (paperback)
ISBN 978 1 4744 9988 0 (webready PDF)
ISBN 978 1 4744 9989 7 (epub)

For Roger Sales (1949–2022)
Scholar, mentor, friend

Contents

Figures

Acknowledgements

This book has been written in order to enhance and enrich the knowledge of students whose interests lie in the field of Victorian Studies specifically, and the study of the long nineteenth century more broadly. It is to the many students whom I have taught over almost thirty years in the English university system and, more recently, at the University of Macau, China, that my profound gratitude must therefore be first expressed. The insight provided by these talented individuals in the seminar room both shapes and tempers those ideas which eventually find concrete expression in books, in book chapters, in journal articles and through conference presentations or symposia. In particular, I would very much like to thank the following former students, who must stand as representatives of the considerable body whom I have taught or whose doctoral theses I have supervised over a long career in the UK: Claire Macnamara, Ian Driscoll, Scott Drew, Michelle Falcon, Charline Blissett, Diane Mason, Molly Thompson, Steve Hunt, Alice Herve, Colin Owens, Malcolm Lewty, Sally White, Morgaine Merch Lleuad, the late Zena Williams, Abigail Bailey-Burton, Aidan Horan, Ellen Long-Common, Emma Sparrow, Emmalynne Goold, Emma Stein, Archy Carroll, Ben Noad, Fliss Falconer, Hannah Roy, Jan Fellows, Sheena Gainey, Jenny Lloyd, Sonja Zimmermann, the late Jasmine Goldsmith, Lauren Brimble, Beverley Douglas, Jenny Patterson, Stuart Coulson, Cathy Poole, Oliver Robinson-Sivyer, Sadie Bennett, Aaron Wilkins, Amber Huckle, the late Hamish Ratley, Becky Spicer, Zara Preston, Leah Morris, Will Purbrook, Margherita Paone, Holly Ryan, Kathy Ewins, Emily Lumbard, Bryony Curass, Ffion Davies and Rebecca Davey. Among my recent students in Macao, I would like to express my gratitude particularly to Jan Marvin Goh, Polina Zhikhar, Quan Yongyu, Xiao Xue, Chan Weng Si, Wang Ruining, Zhou Jiajia, Xia Yuan,

Bonnie de Assis Lew, Firmina Cardoso Gonçalves, Diana Bautista and – especially – Zhang Qingheng.

I am also incredibly grateful for the support and encouragement I have consistently received from friends and colleagues within the Faculty of Arts and Humanities at the University of Macau. In this respect, I would like to thank, in particular, Nick Groom, Matthew Gibson, Damian Shaw, Chiu Man Yin, Andrew Moody, Glenn Timmermans and Yifeng Sun. My sincere thanks also go to Victoria Harrison, Rhett Gale, Jeremy de Chavez, Younhee Kim, Katrine Wong, You Chengcheng and Fei Chen. Tina Chao and Zoe Wong, as always, have been consistently supportive and I would like to thank them, too, for their tolerant good humour.

Outside of Macao, I must also acknowledge the particular support which I received from Jillian Wingfield and Pat Main, both of whom read drafts of this book at various stages of its development, and who provided insightful commentary upon its style and content. I would like to acknowledge, also, the many colleagues with whom I have discussed various aspects of this and other projects, most notably Ruth Heholt (Falmouth University), John Strachan (Bath Spa University), Alison Younger (University of Sunderland), Andrew Smith (University of Sheffield), Jerrold E. Hogle (University of Arizona), Victor Sage (University of East Anglia), Ben Fisher (University of Mississippi), Kasia Ancuta (Chulalongkorn University), Clayton MacKenzie (Zayed University) and Fiona Peters (Bath Spa University). Any errors in this book are, of course, my own. Finally, I am especially grateful to the dedicated and professional team at Edinburgh University Press and extend my particular thanks to Jackie Jones, to Susannah Butler and to Michelle Houston, and also to Robert Tuesley Anderson for his meticulous proofreading. Gillian, as always, deserves my thanks for her support throughout this project, and indeed the other publications on which I have been working at the same time.

This book is dedicated to the memory of one of my oldest and closest friends in academia. I first met Roger Sales in 1982, on the day on which he interviewed me for an undergraduate place at the University of East Anglia, Norwich. I little realised on that occasion how much he would influence my attitude to literary and historical scholarship, and the tenor and style of both my teaching and my writing. I would not be writing this book now, nor teaching at the University of Macau, had it not been for his advice and encouragement over the past forty years. I miss him, terribly. To you, Roger – inspirational scholar, true and honest friend – I extend my deepest thanks.

William Hughes, Cambridge

Figure 1 Map of the British Isles (1842).

Introduction

The poet, dramatist and essayist T. S. Eliot (1888–1965), whose personal commitment to literary Modernism placed him very much in reaction to the aesthetics associated with the century of his birth, was an acute commentator upon the innate fragility of language. In 'Burnt Norton' (1936), the first of his *Four Quartets*, Eliot noted, with staccato relish, how

> . . . Words strain,
> Crack and sometimes break, under the burden,
> Under the tension, slip, slide, perish,
> Decay with imprecision, will not stay in place,
> Will not stay still. . . .[1]

Such an emphatic statement, the implications of which might indeed be applied to every evolving language, has a particular resonance for those who seek to study the Victorian period specifically – or who wish to extend their researches further into its greater context, the so-called long nineteenth century. The Victorian period, its words, conventions and discourses, is, perplexingly for such scholars, both historically close and conceptually distant, forming an uncanny bricolage of the past and the present, of alternating familiarity and strangeness, of once-mundane things turned curiously mythological when englobed in the gaze of a later historical period.

For those students of the nineteenth century who are physically based in the United Kingdom, the Victorian era persists as a constant and evocative backdrop to everyday life: municipal buildings, whether decayed or repurposed for the current century, speak hesitantly of cities whose economic focus and industrial viability have shifted fundamentally in a post-imperial and post-industrial world. The faded formality of public parks and the elaborate architecture of grand railway stations, the elegant iron-and-glass frameworks of the latter sometimes obscured by Brutalist concrete or garish synthetic cladding, testify that all was not utilitarian in the long reign of Victoria, that the functional might satisfactorily coexist with the decorative in the making of an harmonic whole. The devil, as the popular saying would have it, is in the detail. For those who view Victorian infrastructure and nineteenth-century artefacts with twenty-first-century eyes, the rich symbolism that is so-often applied to the visible surface of buildings and objects may as likely provoke questions as provide the reassurance of answers: why should the beehive feature so prominently in the public iconography of the Freemasons, the Oddfellows and the Co-operative Movement, or the bee itself have been chosen as an emblem of Victorian Manchester in 1842? Why does the façade of St Pancras station in London resemble a Gothic abbey but the train-shed it conceals allude so obviously to the Crystal Palace of 1851? Indeed, if the ostensible *meaning* of places and objects may so easily be obscured or else wholly lost in the passage of time, so too might the application or utility of many once-common artefacts in Victorian domesticity or industrial production: the lorgnette has no ophthalmic application in the twenty-first century, and Britannia metal is now seldom deployed in British manufacturing. Again, few gentlemen would consider carrying an ashplant when out walking, and both Mrs Grundy and Mudie's have loosened their once-tenacious hold over literary style and public morality. T. S. Eliot's observation in 'Burnt Norton' is indeed apposite: these – and many other – words, phrases and concepts which underwrote everyday Victorian thought and communication may not have actually perished but now exist only in a debased and imprecise form, casting nothing more than a shadow of their former selves.

The modern associations which have effectively overwritten the contemporary contexts of so many Victorian concepts, objects and gestures of social meaningfulness, might better serve as an index of how cultural commentators in the twentieth and twenty-first centuries have sought to redefine the past as nothing more than an oppositional counterpart for the present. The process by which Victorian conceptuality became essentially uncanny – that is, simultaneously recognisable and yet troublingly dissonant from customary expectation – is perhaps best contemplated with reference to Michel Foucault's modelling of the relationship between the twentieth century and its immediate historical predecessor in *La Volonté de savoir* (1976).

Tellingly retitled *The History of Sexuality: An Introduction* in its 1978 English translation – in part, admittedly, in homage to the three-volume philosophical survey which it ostensibly introduces – Foucault's provocative study of mutability in sexual discourse has implications far beyond its charting of the uneasy relationship between the erotic and the reproductive, and the associated demarcation of the pleasurable from the purposeful.[2] Foucault's thesis is based upon a vision of repression which exceeds the psychoanalytical definition of that term. Acknowledging the pervasive cultural myth which, for the 1960s and 1970s, defined the nineteenth century through the still-abiding memory – perhaps, even, the enduring presence – of 'the imperial prude', Foucault deconstructed the whole edifice of contemporary cultural liberation as being founded upon nothing more than a 'restrained, mute, and *hypocritical* sexuality'.[3] The twentieth century, Foucault argues, necessarily defined the nineteenth century as a period characterised by a prudish avoidance of sexuality in order to enforce its own claim to a 'liberated' frankness in sexual discourse. That which the Victorians were unable to vocalise was the very essence of the subject which the now-'liberated' peoples of contemporary Europe constantly narrated in their writings, represented graphically across their dramatic media, and practised, openly and promiscuously, in their private – or, perhaps, it might be said, gratuitously public – lives.

As Foucault argues, repression is an aspect of power – and to inscribe repression as the defining practice of a supposedly eclipsed culture is to impose power rhetorically upon the past in the interests of the present. Victorian individuals, of course, proclaimed their sexuality – or, perhaps, their polyvalent sexualities – in much the same way as their counterparts in the twentieth and twenty-first centuries: in the form of personal testimony; by way of fiction and other arts; through modes of dress, and subtle gestures of affirmation or recognition; and as expressions of conformity to, as much as of rebellion against, convention. The processes of coding and signalling through which such dissonances were permitted a form of semi-covert expression in orthodox culture have their parallels in the modern world, where certain subjects and attitudes may apparently not be openly voiced for fear of censure or – to use a fashionable expression – the 'cancelling' of an individual, text or opinion in the interests of contemporary culture. Liberation and vocalisation may well be achieved at the cultural cost of a new culture of repression and silencing, imposed reciprocally and at the further expense of free and interrogative debate. The risk is that *any* identity or belief which is conducted – whether this be wholly or in part – covertly embodies a degree of cultural fragility, a conceptual brittleness which may propel its originating context even further into obscurity.

To extend Foucault's argument about sexuality to the broader subject of how the past – and its concepts, artefacts and ostensible attitudes – may be understood by later historical periods, the Victorian period has, in recent years, been pushed to further alienation not simply as a consequence of its apparently repressive attitude towards recreational sex but also on account of its perceived relationship to other issues distasteful and inimical to twenty-first-century values. Hence, the nineteenth century becomes the repository and expression of those institutionalised prejudices whose consequences are readily perceived in the social and cultural inequities and environmental degradations of the global twenty-first century. As a historical period premised upon the lucrative commercialism of Anglo-Saxon (or at least European) imperialists, the Victorian era may thus be contemplated as a period in which the racist inequalities of historical slavery were perpetuated rather than properly corrected, the consequences of the slave trade persisting as a legacy still to be addressed in the twenty-first century by the descendants of traders and traded alike.[4] Similarly, the same ruthless commercialism might be associated with the environmental indifference of the Victorians at home and abroad, or at least with their ignorance of ecological consequences whose implications were fully comprehended only with the opening of a compelling debate upon climate change and its relationship to the ethics of industrial development.[5] The pervasive sexism of the nineteenth century, supported as it was by the gendered authorities of medicine and science, likewise forms a barrier which perceptibly separates Victorian culture from modernity, while an inflexible and inequitable model of social class is perceived by some commentators as having – remarkably – preserved the puissance of an anachronistic elite far beyond its supposed heyday. Such preoccupations, tempting and evocative as they are, do much the same work as Foucault's hypothetical Victorian prude: they say more about the present, perhaps, than they do about the past, and their insistent struggle for intellectual or moral pre-eminence increasingly configures the nineteenth century as the conceptual and generalised antithesis of the twenty-first, insisting that it can only make sense when viewed in terms of its imperfections, those things from which the perceiving century may proclaim its own conceptual liberation, its own self-conscious distance. To actually *engage* with the past, one must necessarily be aware of how the philosophical and cultural institutions of the perceiving present shape perception and interpretation.

To return again to *The History of Sexuality: An Introduction*, Foucault closes his opening chapter by suggesting that the work which follows aspires to bypass the distraction of 'the repressive hypothesis, and the facts of interdiction or exclusion it invokes' through the foregrounding of 'certain historical facts that serve as guidelines for research'.[6] While the definition of what may justifiably be termed a 'fact', and how such 'facts' might be verified to the satisfaction of a disparate body of readers, remains a contentious one, Foucault's purported strategy would appear to be one calculated to break down – or break through – the monoliths of interpretation. The 'facts' in question are those which might be extracted from the immediate interplay of words and concepts as recorded in historical documentation – in Foucault's case, through a survey of material culture which partially precedes the Victorian period and whose lingering influence may be traced in his own contemporaries' attitude to the nineteenth century.[7] Foucault's 'facts', as it were, are the atomised components 'of discursive production' or – more emphatically – 'of the production of power': they are the components of a cultural grammar, of a network of assumptions, of causes and effects which are not those of a later, perceiving, century. Though in many cases offensive or discordant to modern sensibilities, their logic is nonetheless that of their own time, and their relationship to each other illustrates the mechanisms, the opinions and preoccupations that generate them.[8]

A degree of insight regarding this logic – dissonant though it may so often be to modern tastes and beliefs – is surely essential to any serious scholar of the Victorian period. Victorian studies, as an academic discipline, requires if not a participation in the thought of that period then at least a guarded and critical empathy – and a willingness to pursue context far beyond a merely superficial contemplation. Such an engagement is not possible without a sustained attention to detail, and a consideration of what the 'facts' or artefacts under consideration actually meant to a *Victorian* perceiver as well as to an interpreter or commentator who is grounded in the consciousness of the twenty-first century. It is true that explanations of this type are frequently incorporated into the selective notes that punctuate academic editions of Victorian novels. Similar insights, again, are often deployed to support the conclusions reached by both sober bio-graphical writings and more imaginative speculations regarding the behaviour or motivations of historical individuals. These intimations, though, driven as they are by the necessity of illuminating elements of a specific text or else accentuating some aspect of a biographical study, are characteristically economic with regard to depth of cover-age. For the student or general reader whose literary interests range more widely across a number of nineteenth-century fictions, or whose need to survey a historical event or tendency will involve them in a protracted engagement with archival documentation or newspaper reportage, a different type of reference work is needed: one whose definitions are premised upon primary sources, one which will further point the enquirer to contemplate related issues or relevant legisla-tion, one which is comprehensive and structured in such a way as to facilitate its deployment as a resource across a broad, rather than narrow, field of study. The present volume – significantly titled *Key Concepts in Victorian Studies* – aspires to fulfil such a function, and to serve as an accessible reference work that will support the studies undertaken by individual readers and researchers at all levels of engagement with the culture of the nineteenth century.

How to Use This Book

Key Concepts in Victorian Studies differs in a number of significant ways from the earlier volumes published in this well-established series. The functional heart of *Key Concepts in Victorian Studies* – an alphabetically ordered glossary of specifically Victorian words, phrases and concepts, supported through detailed reference to con-textual matter such as historical events and formal legislation – is considerably larger than those to be found within the other volumes in the series. The detailed definitions which populate this meticulously cross-referenced glossary are further clarified through the book's incorporation of a range of carefully selected illustrations, sourced primarily from nineteenth-century publications. To enable the reader to contextualise their own particular interests within the period, *Key Concepts in Victorian Studies* includes, in addition, a detailed chrono-logical survey of the domestic, imperial and international preoccupa-tions which characterised each year of the reign of Queen Victoria. Further historical context is provided by way of a table of the prime ministers of the United Kingdom of Great Britain and Ireland during the Queen's sixty-three-year reign, with details of the premier's political affiliation and period in office being supplied in each case. This party political timeline is further supplemented by a survey of the most significant legislation enacted by Parliament between 1837 and 1901 – a unique contextual resource which will afford the reader a detailed but succinct insight into the breadth of domestic policy as manifested in those Acts of Parliament which addressed, in particular, employment, poverty, health, education, and religious observance in an era of unprecedented social change. The final two sections of *Key Concepts in Victorian Studies* will assist the reader's comprehension of both pre-decimal British currency and of the imperial system of measurement which preceded the wholesale adoption of metric measurement in the twentieth century.

Key Concepts in Victorian Studies has thus been designed as a durable work of reference, the contents of which will support scholars of nineteenth-century domestic and imperial history as well as readers of Victorian fiction, poetry and drama. The central glossary of terms and concepts has been structured alphabetically so as to facilitate access to definitions which are succinct, authoritative and quotable. Where a term or concept is associated with an alternative or colloquial name, these latter are listed separately in the glossary and the reader is directed to the context provided by the main entry. The glossary, indeed, has been specifically designed to allow connections to be made between entries through systematic cross-referencing. Cross-references throughout are given in **bold**. The dates of birth and death for authors, poets, dramatists, politicians and other historical figures are provided in parentheses within each entry, as is the date of first appearance for any named publication.

The individual entries which make up the glossary cover the breadth of Victorian culture in that they address and acknowledge such crucial fields as faith and spirituality, domestic and imperial manners, the formalities of military and civilian life, and the tenor of popular radicalism as well as the more formal politics of monarchy and Parliament. At a basic level, the glossary will greatly assist the reader to understand the import of the many once-familiar domestic words and phrases which have simply disappeared from modern vocabulary, but whose effective ghosts still populate those Victorian fictions widely read both within and beyond academia. It will, further, highlight the penetration of words of colonial origin into everyday English, acknowledging the prejudices and assumptions which these embody through original context rather than the polemic of the twenty-first century. It will be evident that many of the terms mentioned in the glossary precede the nineteenth century or else remain in use – sometimes in a modified but identifiable form – in the twenty-first. This situation is, of course, unavoidable in a work which seeks to clarify *any* broad historical period. The conventions of the Victorian period necessarily make reference to those which preceded them, just as the twenty-first century unavoidably acknowledges its temporal predecessor.

For this reason – and because so many of these conventions are rendered almost transparent by their ostensible familiarity – the glossary is deliberate in its clarification of, for example, the social precedence which distinguishes the various titles held by the English, Scots and Irish peerage, the specific duties performed by the different clerical offices within the Church of England, and the function of several now-obsolete ranks within the armed forces. In addition to this, the glossary provides a full explanation for many of the most common abbreviations which punctuate Victorian fiction, reportage and letters. These include academic, political, military and social prefixes and postnomial designations, abbreviated and Latinate terms deployed in formal business and legal correspondence, and contracted words or phrases used in colloquial exchanges.

The disciplines of medicine and law – with their freighting of technical, abbreviated and Latinate terminology – are necessarily acknowledged in *Key Concepts in Victorian Studies*. In the case of the former, the glossary is systematic in its explanation of the clinical and social distinctions that existed within a medical profession divided as much by the class and relative wealth of the patient as by the ostensible specialism of the practitioner. Beyond this, the glossary acknowledges the practices of self-diagnosis and self-medication by way of named patent medicines, and outlines also the pathology and treatment associated with the most commonly encountered diseases and disorders of nineteenth-century life. Those practices such as mesmerism and phrenology, which came to be dismissed as pseudosciences as the nineteenth century progressed towards its fin de siècle, are also noted. In parallel to its treatment of medicine, the glossary likewise describes the professional distinctions that denominate the practitioners of English and Scots law, notes the intimacy between ecclesiastical and civil jurisprudence, explains the legal basis of inheritance, and also the distinctions which structure marriage in England

and Scotland. The subcultural worlds of the criminal rookeries and waterside opium dens, with their distinctive slang, are also acknowledged in many of the entries within the glossary.

In addition to its coverage of Victorian professional life, the glossary is comprehensive in its contemplation of those leisured pursuits which might be enjoyed in the evening or at the weekend. The development of team sports is noted by way of both amateur and professional competition, as is the influence of those bodies which appointed themselves as the authors or arbiters of rules and discipline. The meanings of technical terms commonplace within the field sports of hunting and shooting are also clarified, and the latter activities are further related to the social calendar associated with both the country life of the upper classes and the elaborate ritual of the London season. With regard to proletarian life, the characteristic features of popular theatrical entertainment are explained, as are the rival attractions presented by the gin palace and the Salvation Army citadel. That most formal of Victorian social rituals, the public funeral – with its characteristic and ostentatious public displays of morality and dignity – is also explored in detail through a number of entries within the glossary.

The glossary is further distinguished by the particular attention which has been paid to parliamentary legislation across the century. Each individual act of Parliament mentioned in the glossary is described briefly therein and cross-referenced, where appropriate, to the more detailed entries to be found in the subsequent survey of significant legislation. The descriptions provided in both sections, though, are further augmented by the inclusion of the unique formal citation which is legally associated with each individual piece of legislation. Provided in each case in parentheses in the compressed format that was used in the nineteenth century – for example, the 1870 *Married Women's Property Act* would be cited as 33 & 34 Vict. c. 93 – these acts may thus be researched further, and in many cases their original content retrieved, through the facilities afforded by several authoritative online – and open-access – resources including, in the United Kingdom, the National Archives, the record of parliamentary debates that is *Hansard*, and Parliament's own website.[9] Where a short entry in the glossary has a more detailed counterpart in the survey of significant legislation, its parenthesised citation will be highlighted in bold type and underlined, thus: (**33 & 34 Vict. c. 93**).

Victorian studies, with its disciplinary integration of literature, history and political thought, has historically functioned as one of the core disciplines of a liberal education. That this relatively narrow historical period, its perceived attitudes and documented personalities, continue to provoke lively – and, at times, heated – debate is surely testament to its enduring value within modern intellectual culture. As the nineteenth century recedes into more distant history, though, and as its physical monuments crumble or are torn down, there is a distinct risk that the culture of the Victorian period will become less and less accessible in the future. *Key Concepts in Victorian Studies*, it is to be hoped, will in a small way assist the next generation of scholars to distinguish and appreciate the fascinating paradoxes of this formative period in recent history through an enhanced understanding of its most basic concepts and their expression in literature, legislation and the conventions of social and political life. The relatively compact format of *Key Concepts in Victorian Studies* should therefore not be taken as an index of its coverage. Like that staple of Victorian domestic bookshelves, *Enquire Within upon Everything* – a publication which, of course, may be found in the glossary – *Key Concepts in Victorian Studies* will prove a durable, portable and, above all, authoritative resource that is rich in both contextual detail and accessible explanation.

Notes

1. T. S. Eliot, 'Burnt Norton' V, in *The Complete Plays and Poems of T. S. Eliot* (London: Faber & Faber, 1970), pp. 171–83 at p. 175.
2. Michel Foucault, *The History of Sexuality: An Introduction*, trans. Robert Hurley (New York: Pantheon, 1978), p. 4. *La Volonté de savoir* translates literally as 'the will to knowledge', and is the first volume of *L'Histoire de la sexualité* (*The History of Sexuality*), the remaining volumes being *L'Usage des plaisirs* (1984, translated in 1985 as *The Use of Pleasure*) and *Le Souci de soi* (1984, translated in 1986 as *The Care of the Self*). A fourth volume, *Les Aveux de la chair*, was published posthumously in French in 2018, and in English as *Confessions of the Flesh* in 2022.
3. Foucault, *The History of Sexuality: An Introduction*, p. 3, my emphasis.
4. Witness the controversy which accompanied the visit of the Duke and Duchess of Cambridge to the former British colonies of the Caribbean in March 2022. See: Moya Lothian-McLean, 'After that disastrous royal tour, is the sun finally setting on the Commonwealth realms?', *The*

Guardian, 27 March 2022, available online at https://www.theguardian.com/uk-news/2022/mar/27/royal-tour-commonwealth-queen-elizabeth-william-kate-caribbean, accessed 31 March 2022.

5. See, for example, Wendy Parkins and Peter Adkins, 'Introduction: Victorian Ecology and the Anthropocene', *19: Interdisciplinary Studies in the Long Nineteenth Century* (2018) 26, 1–15, available online at https://19.bbk.ac.uk/article/id/1717/, accessed 31 March 2022.

6. Foucault, *The History of Sexuality: An Introduction*, p. 13.

7. Foucault, *The History of Sexuality: An Introduction*, p. 10.

8. Foucault, *The History of Sexuality: An Introduction*, p. 12.

9. The National Archives maintains a searchable online database – which covers much of the legislation enacted between 1267 and the present – on behalf of the UK Government at https://www.legislation.gov.uk/. The official parliamentary website (https://www.parliament.uk/), while being concerned primarily with contemporary legislation, may also be searched for revisions of earlier Acts of Parliament, while *Hansard* (https://hansard.parliament.uk/), the formal record of proceedings in Parliament, can be searched for quotable information on the speeches and debates which accompanied each proposal in the Houses of Lords and Commons as well as their later revisions. Websites accessed on 22 March 2022.

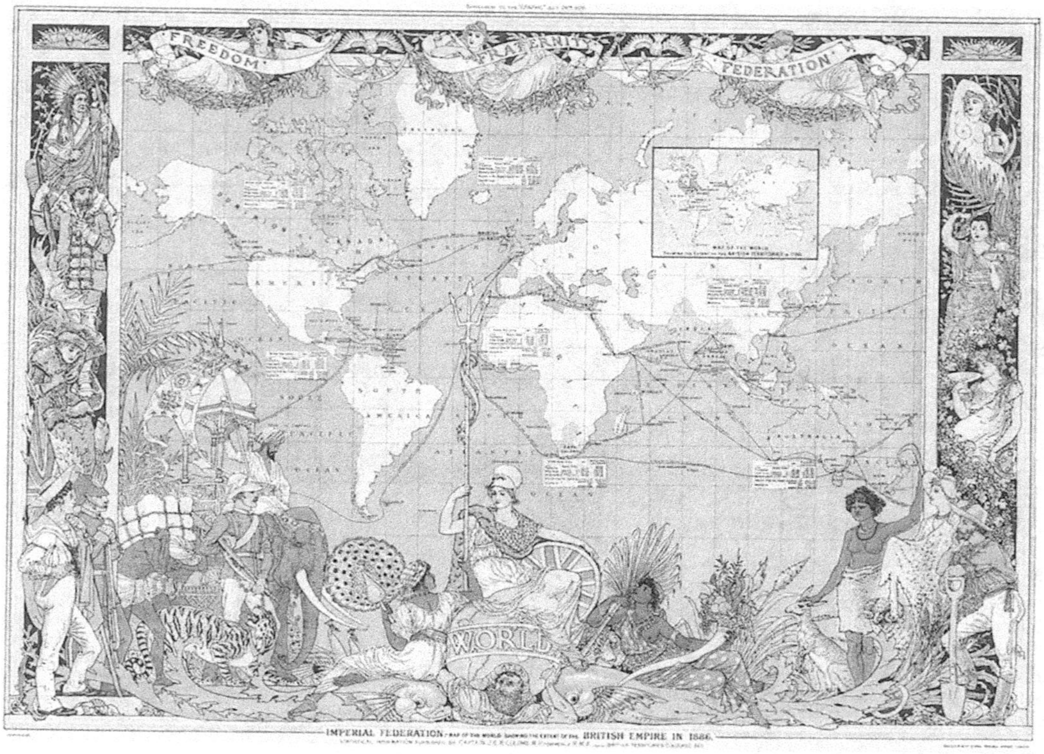

Figure 2 The British Empire in 1886: supplement to *The Graphic*, 24 July 1886

A–Z of Key Concepts and Terms

AB A post-nominal abbreviation of the Latin phrase *Artium Bacca-laureus* which signifies that its possessor is a Bachelor of Arts (BA). See also: **AM**.

abortion Illegal in Britain under the provisions of the 1803 *Malicious Shooting Act* (43 Geo. 3 c. 58), the essentially Christian prohi-bition of abortion was further enhanced by the 1861 *Offences Against the Person Act* (<u>24 & 25 Vict. c. 100</u>). This latter crimi-nalised the procuring or administration of drugs or instruments by which a pregnancy might be terminated. Despite this legisla-tion, chemical abortifacients – often termed 'female pills' – could be easily obtained from dispensing chemists or through news-paper advertisements, and midwives often administered illegal physical terminations at home.

absentee landlords Non-resident landowners who employ a factor or agent to collect rent on their behalf. In Irish context, the land-owners were often **Protestant**, the tenants **Roman Catholic**, and disputes over the relative cost of tenancy and availability of land inflected with sectarian hostility. In Ireland, the perceived excesses of landlordism led to the establishment of an active Land League from 1879, and to local rent strikes, **boycotts** and, on occasion, arson or violence.

absinthe A psychoactive and alcoholic drink associated with **decadence** and the **fin-de-siècle** cult of the **aesthete**. Though popular with all social classes in France, absinthe never eclipsed gin as a demotic drink in late-Victorian Britain.

accouchement A term used in both medical discourse and polite com-pany to signify the period in which a woman is customarily 'confined' in order to give birth.

Adullamites An anti-Reform faction within the **Liberal Party**, active between 1866 and 1867, and opposed to any further widening of the elective franchise. The name alludes to the Cave of Adullam in the Old Testament (1 Samuel 22).

adulteration The deliberate contamination and bulking of foodstuffs, usually undertaken in order to enhance the profit of the vendor. Milk was often diluted with water (thus potentially exposing the drinker to the **cholera** morbus), flour compromised with alum or chalk, copper or **arsenic** added to pickles to enhance colour, and lead incorporated as a sweetener in wine and **port**. Con-tamination was also latent in the processing of many liquids, as sheet lead was frequently utilised to line fermenting or storage containers.

adultery Because marriage was frequently imbricated with issues of property, adultery must be understood as having significant legal as well as moral and religious implications. Under the 1857 *Matrimonial Causes Act* (<u>**20 & 21 Vict. c. 85**</u>), a husband could **divorce** his wife for adultery alone, though a wife would need to prove in addition a compounding offence such as bigamy, cruelty, desertion or incest.

Aestheticism A loosely organised cultural movement active between c. 1860 and 1900 which drew upon ideas expressed within both the **Arts and Crafts movement** and **Pre-Raphaelitism**. Aestheticism was premised upon a rejection of the purposeful materialism of the industrial age in favour of a doctrine of 'Art for Art's Sake'. In art and design, Aestheticism favoured sensuality in colour, image and texture, and in writing generated a nuanced avant-garde manner in which style often predominated over substance. Frequently mocked for its perceived elitism and pretentiousness, Aestheticism was also often associated with **homosexuality** and sexual radicalism, and thus was negatively impacted by the trial, in 1895, of Oscar Wilde (1854–1900), one of its popular figureheads.

Afghanistan A mountainous region bordering the Punjab, regarded as being of strategic significance due to of the access it afforded to India by way of the **Khyber** and Bolan Passes.

Albany Sometimes 'The Albany', a prestigious collection of bachelor apartments – known as 'sets' – located in London's Piccadilly.

albert The chain by which a gentleman's pocket watch may be secured to his waistcoat so as to prevent its theft by pickpockets.

Albertopolis An area of South Kensington, developed as a focus of cultural and intellectual life in London by Albert, the **Prince Consort** (1819–61) and Sir Henry Cole (1808–82) following the **Great Exhibition**. It accommodates the Royal Albert Hall (opened 1871), Natural History Museum (opened 1881) and the Royal College of Music (established 1882). The Victoria and Albert Museum was instituted as a museum of manufactures in 1852, the foundation stone of the current building being formally laid by Queen Victoria in 1899.

alienist A medical practitioner who specialises in mental illness and who, in the capacity of a medico-jurist, may on occasion be called to present an opinion in legal proceedings.

AM A post-nominal abbreviation of the Latin term *Artium Magister*, which denotes that an individual possesses the university degree of Master of Arts (MA). In the Universities of Oxford, Cambridge and Dublin, the Master's degree might be conferred upon the holder of a BA without further study at a period subsequent to his graduation. See also: **AB**.

anaesthesia Prior to the development of chemical anaesthesia, surgery was often undertaken on conscious patients who were physically restrained by the surgeon's assistants. Though **mesmerism** and **hypnotism** were occasionally deployed to relieve pain and restrict spasmodic movement during surgery, inhalational techniques were introduced from the 1840s. Nitrous oxide was administered in the United States as early as 1844, and **ether** was utilised in Britain for dental surgery and amputations in 1846 before being applied as an analgesic in midwifery in 1847. **Chloroform** was introduced in 1847, and its administration to Queen Victoria as a childbirth analgesic in 1853 did much to popularise its use as a pain-reliever in surgery.

anarchism Though a specifically British tradition of theoretical anarchism can be traced to the radical writings of William Godwin (1756–1836), the arrival in Britain of political activists displaced by the European revolutions of 1848 underwrote its presence as an international movement within the English capital. Though on occasions associated with violent actions – a bomb exploded in Greenwich Park in 1894, killing the anarchist who carried it – British anarchism lacked a unifying focus beyond a nebulous vision of social and political change.

Anglican A member of the Church of England, the state-endorsed **Protestant** Christian denomination in England, Wales and Ireland until its disestablishment in Ireland in 1871 and in Wales in 1914. The Anglican Church is Episcopalian (governed by **bishops**), and its comparative wealth – gathered historically in the form of tithes paid by members of all religious denominations – as well as political influence (Anglican bishops sat as legislators in the **House of Lords**) made it unpopular with Protestant **dissenters** and **Roman Catholics** as well as those advocating a secular society. See also: **Church of Scotland**; *Crockford's*; **Oxford Movement**; **Tractarianism**.

Anglo-Catholic See: **Oxford Movement**; **Tractarian**.

antisepsis Despite the advances in pain relief which accompanied the deployment of chemical **anaesthetics**, patients remained vulnerable to infection transmitted by contaminated hands, instruments and dressings as well as the bodily fluids of those who had earlier occupied the operating table. Influenced by the germ theories of Louis Pasteur (1822–95), Joseph Lister (1827–1912) encouraged the use of a weak carbolic acid as a handwash and as an antiseptic vapour surrounding the patient from around 1867, thus significantly reducing morbid infection. A more comprehensive regime of aseptic surgery, which included the gowning of clinicians, was initiated in the 1890s.

apothecary A general medical practitioner. Apothecaries were generally less prestigious and thus cheaper to consult than **physicians** or **surgeons**. Historically, apothecaries were regulated by the Apothecaries' Society of London or the Apothecaries' Hall of Ireland, though many practised without licence prior to the *Medical Act* of 1858 (**21 & 22 Vict. c. 90**). This latter confirmed each duly registered apothecary as 'a legally qualified Medical Practitioner', and debarred 'unregistered persons' from obtaining formal medical appointments within most civil and military establishments.

apprentice An individual who is bound by an indenture – a legal agreement or contract – to serve under an experienced craftsperson or professional for a set period of time in order to learn that craft or profession. Apprenticeships could last as long as seven years and were often initiated by parents or, in the case of orphans, **workhouse** guardians. Apprentices – sometimes undeservedly, no doubt – enjoyed a reputation for idleness, drunkenness and excess when not under the direct supervision of their employer.

arcades Covered shopping thoroughfares, in many respects similar to the Parisian *passages*, and usually associated – at the time of opening, at least – with the sale of luxury goods. The earliest examples in Britain – such as the Royal Opera Arcade (1818) and the **Lowther Arcade** (1830), both in London – were opened prior to the accession of Queen Victoria. Surviving Victorian examples include Thornton's Arcade (1878), Leeds; the Morgan Arcade (1896), Cardiff; Wayfarer's Arcade (1898), Southport; and the **art nouveau** Royal Arcade (1899), Norwich.

archery Revived as a nationally organised sport towards mid-century, but popular since at least the 1830s, archery was a pastime in which men and women could complete with something approaching

Figure 3 Thomas Crane, 'Lowther Arcade' from Thomas Crane and Ellen Houghton, *London Town* (1883).

equality. Archery tournaments provided social and romantic opportunities for their primarily middle-class participants and spectators, as well as an opportunity to encounter noble – and on occasion royal – patrons of toxophily.

'Arriet and 'Arry A generic **Cockney** couple, prone to slang and boisterous behaviour, popularised from the 1870s by way of the editorial prose of Edwin James Milliken (1839–97) in *Punch* and through cartoons drawn for the periodical by George du Maurier (1834–96) and Phil May (1864–1903). 'Arry's colloquial remarks and mode of dress characteristically mocked not merely contemporary working-class manners but also the upper-class affectations which they supposedly aped.

arsenic A poisonous chemical element, arsenic was none the less widely incorporated in medicines, as a food colouring, in cosmetics, and as a pigment in the production of vividly green, blue and **yellow** wallpaper and textiles. Arsenic trioxide, in the form of an almost tasteless white powder that could be purchased routinely from chemists and grocery shops, was commonly used as a domestic poison for the eradication of vermin such as rats and mice. The easy availability of this latter, under various commercial names, gained it the reputation of the poison of choice in murders, given that the symptoms it produced – vomiting and diarrhoea – were almost indistinguishable from accidental food poisoning. The availability of arsenic was restricted by the 1851 *Sale of Arsenic Regulation Act* (14 & 15 Vict. c. 13). See also: **adulteration**.

art nouveau A **fin-de-siècle** style in graphic and sculptural art, in ceramics and metalwork, and in furniture and architecture, art nouveau characteristically draws upon the sensuality and sinuosity of organic form, favouring intricacy of design and a tonal palette that often deploys vivid shades of **yellow** and green as well as darker touches of red and blue. Though often associated with European **decadence** and the **greenery-yallery** of **Aestheticism**, British art nouveau was heavily influenced by the **Arts and Crafts movement** and the circle of Scottish designers popularly known as the **Glasgow School**.

articled clerk A trainee solicitor, usually without a university degree, who is studying law while working in a legal office. 'Reading for Articles' over a period of around five years was considered a less prestigious, though far cheaper, route to legal qualification, and did not require a protracted residence in London.

Arts and Crafts movement An idealistic and loose movement, initiated in the 1880s, which prioritised the values, style and durability associated with traditional crafts and rejected the cultures of industrial mass production in favour of small-scale artisanship. Aesthetically, Arts and Crafts style eschewed the superfluous decoration of earlier Victorian products, and favoured purposeful simplicity and the quirky irregularities that might be associated with small-scale or artisan production. Its influence was greatest in the manufacture of ceramics, furniture and woodwork, textiles for decoration and fashion, printing and bookbinding, and to some extent architecture. Though the name 'Arts and Crafts' (which is derived from the title of a society founded in 1887) may be used to distinguish the movement generally, its various creative components were essentially discrete, and their products marketed either by quasi-fraternal organisations such as the Art Workers' Guild (founded 1884) or through design-and-production enterprises such as Morris and Company (founded 1861, re-founded 1875) and retailers such as Liberty of London (established 1875). William Morris (1834–96) was a pivotal figure in the movement, balancing a past implicated in the colourful medievalism of **Pre-Raphaelitism** and anticipating the **fin-de-siècle** taste for **art nouveau**. See also: **Glasgow School.**

ashplant Sometimes hyphenated as ash-plant, a light walking stick or flexible goad made from the wood of the ash tree.

assizes The Courts of Assize were periodic meetings in which legal cases were decided by a jury in the presence of a peripatetic judge. This latter would be one of several legal professionals presiding over a specific 'circuit' of law courts held in provincial towns and cities, with trials often being conducted in public buildings which also served as town or county halls where no purpose-built courtroom existed.

association football A separate game from the older **rugby football**, the sport became formally organised in 1863 with the foundation of the Football Association: 'soccer', an alternative name for the game, is a colloquialism derived from 'Association', just as 'rugger' is a colloquialism of rugby. Professional (as opposed to amateur) football was authorised by the Football Association in 1885; rugby, by contrast, retained a formal institutional commitment to amateur sportsmanship for a decade beyond this.

at home A social custom, in which the presiding lady of the a middle- or upper-class house advised her friends that she would be available for them to call on her 'at home' on a predetermined afternoon in order to take tea and engage in polite conversation. Cards were printed for this purpose, and distributed in advance: to visit without such an invitation was considered at best a social faux pas and at worst an act of presumption. See also: **calling card.**

Athenæum Club Founded in Pall Mall, London, in 1824, the Athenæum is a gentlemen's club, the members of which were elected upon the basis of their achievements rather than social origins or political affiliation. Its membership embraced the arts and the sciences: Charles Dickens (1812–70) and Charles Darwin (1809–82) were elected to membership on the same day in 1838.

atmospheric railway An experimental **railway**, designed by Isambard Kingdom Brunel (1806–59), which utilised air pressure rather than locomotives to move passengers. Though technologically advanced, the necessary vacuum was vulnerable to drops in pressure, and the line ran for less than a year, being converted to conventional steam operation in 1848.

ayah A native-born female **servant**, particularly one employed in colonial India for the everyday care of European children.

B

baccarat A card game played between two hands, the 'banker' and the 'player'. Sir William Gordon-Cumming (1848–1930), an associate of the **Prince of Wales**, was named in a gambling scandal – the Tranby Croft affair – in 1891, his act of cheating at baccarat costing him his position in the army and his respectability within fashionable London society. See also: **chemin de fer**.

bad form A polite but colloquial description of behaviour or manners which offend or else fail to satisfy the current standard.

Baedeker Any of a series of guidebooks issued by the Coblenz publisher Karl Baedeker (1801–59) from the late 1820s. Though early Baedekers were published in German, anglophone guides were issued from the 1860s. See also: *Bradshaw's*.

Balmorality Derived from the residence of Queen Victoria and Prince Albert at Balmoral Castle, Aberdeenshire, this term denotes a romanticised attitude to Scotland generally and to the distinctive manners, dress and culture of the Scottish Highlands in particular. Royal patronage of Scottish culture from 1842 did much to make the Highlands fashionable in the eyes of tourists as well as those involved in **field sports** such as **grouse shooting** and **deer stalking**, and generated a further interest in the collecting and display of **Tartanware** and similar souvenirs.

Band of Hope A **temperance** organisation for children, founded in Leeds in 1847. Members were encouraged to sign a pledge committing them to abstain from consuming alcoholic intoxicants and often wore medals or blue ribbons to advertise their decision.

bangy-wallah In colonial Indian speech, a porter who carries loads using a bangy or shoulder-yoke. See also: **wallah**.

bank holidays The *Bank Holidays Act* (34 & 35 Vict. c. 17) of 1871 authorised the establishment of four days in England, Wales and

Ireland, and five in Scotland, when commercial business was effectively restricted due to the statutory closure of financial establishments. In England, Wales and Ireland these days were Easter Monday, the first Monday in August, the 26th December and Whit Monday: Good Friday and **Christmas** Day were regarded as traditional days of Christian worship and were not included in the Act. In Scotland, where religious and cultural traditions were somewhat different, the equivalent days were specified as New Year's Day, Good Friday, the first Monday in May, the first Monday in August, and Christmas Day.

Bank of England Founded as a private bank in London in 1694, the Bank of England's control over the issuing of banknotes was enhanced by the *Bank Charter Act* (7 & 8 Vict. c. 32) of 1844. Banknotes, which did not bear the image of the reigning monarch until 1960, were in essence a written promise that the document might be exchanged for **currency** when presented at the bank.

bankruptcy The condition of being unable to pay one's debts had social as well as financial implications across the century. While imprisonment for debt was abolished in 1869, creditors who were owned a significant sum might initiate costly legal action in order to force the sale or disposal of property, though lesser amounts were sometimes forcibly recovered by unregulated debt collectors acting on the part of backstreet moneylenders, and **gombeenmen**. Once insolvency was formally announced in the *London Gazette*, personal credit would become difficult to obtain and a degree of social ostracism would likely follow. See also: **dunn; Fleet Prison; Marshalsea Prison; Queer Street.**

banns An announcement of an intended marriage given in church, whether verbally or by way of a written or printed notice, which provides an opportunity for an objection to be formally raised against the coming ceremony – for example in cases of bigamy or consanguinity. To 'forbid the banns' is to make such an objection against a forthcoming marriage.

Baptist War See: **Jamaica Rebellion.**

baronet The most junior of the hereditary orders of British nobility. A baronet is entitled to the prefix 'Sir', and the post-nominal Baronet, Bart. or Bt. A baronetage is hereditary where a knighthood – which also confers the prefix 'Sir' – is not. See also: **peerage.**

barrister A specialist in legal advocacy who represents individuals or organisations in courts of law. In England, barristers were conventionally trained at, or were members of, one of the four **Inns of Court** in London, and usually held a university degree. See also: **articled clerk; bencher.**

bashi-bazouks Derived from the Turkish word *başibozuk*, an irregular and ill-disciplined body of Ottoman troops that fought during the **Crimean War** and was held accountable for the worst excesses of the **Bulgarian Horrors.**

bathing machine A wheeled cabin used to protect personal modesty while undressing for sea bathing. The bather entered the cabin on the foreshore, and it was wheeled to the edge of the tide, so minimising the time in which the body, when clad in a bathing costume, was visible to bystanders.

beadle A parish officer or constable responsible for administering local justice. The term may also be used to denote a university official or (in Scotland particularly) a church functionary.

beagling A **field sport** in which hares, and on occasion rabbits, are hunted on foot and with a pack of beagles.

beater An individual employed in domestic **pheasant shooting** and **grouse shooting** – as well as in colonial big-game hunting – in order to drive the quarry species towards the **guns**. Though nominally at a distance from the guns, beaters were sometimes injured (or 'peppered') by incautious or inexperienced participants in **field sports.**

beehive The traditional domed 'bee skep' was widely used as an emblem of industry and industriousness, featuring as such in the symbolism of **freemasonry** as well as in the iconography of the **co-operative movement.** The worker bee, similarly, is an emblem of hard work and resilience: it was legally incorporated into the civic arms of Manchester on city status being granted to the borough in 1842.

beer See: **India Pale Ale; porter; small beer.**

bencher A senior member of the legal profession who forms part of the management of one of the **Inns of Court** and has the right to 'call an individual to the Bar' – that is, to formally appoint them a **barrister.**

bicycle The velocipede – a bicycle or tricycle in which the pedals were affixed directly to the axle – was developed in the 1870s, with the dangerously tall **penny farthing** gaining popularity in the 1880s. The so-called 'safety bicycle', which featured simple gears connected to a chain drive and smaller wheels, appeared around 1885.

bill broker One who deals in 'bills of exchange' – promissory notes, associated with debts or deferred payments which will become due at some point in the future.

bill hook A thick agricultural knife with a hooked end, used for pruning or cutting.

billiards An indoor game played on a rectangular baize-covered table, in which three balls, usually of ivory, are struck by the players with a wooden cue. A governing body, the Billiards Association, was founded in 1885. See also: **snooker**.

billycock A round, low-crowned felt hat similar to the bowler or **coke** hat. Ostensibly a male garment, it was occasionally worn by women, particularly the **New Woman**.

bishop In **Anglican** usage, a senior church official who presides over an ecclesiastical diocese. Bishops sat in the **House of Lords**, and in England were subject to the two archbishops of the Church, based in York (Ebor) and Canterbury (Cantuar). **Roman Catholic** bishoprics were established in England in 1850, and in Scotland in 1878. The name is also applied to a hot drink made with wine, port and aromatic spices.

black drop One of a number of **opium**-based medicines frequently deployed to pacify teething babies or else help induce sleep in adults suffering from insomnia.

Blackwood's Edinburgh Magazine A popular monthly magazine, known colloquially as 'Maga', published in Edinburgh from 1817. **Tory** rather than **Whig** in its sympathies, the periodical published original fiction by authors as diverse as James Hogg (1770–1835), Margaret Oliphant (1828–97), George Eliot (1819–80) and Joseph Conrad (1857–1924), as well as articles of topical, cultural and political interest.

blood transfusion Though the **physician** James Blundell (1790–1878) performed a successful transfusion of blood by way of a syringe as early as 1818, the procedure remained inherently risky until three human blood groups were satisfactorily defined in 1901, and the fourth a year later. A more efficient vehicle for the transfusion of blood – the Aveling apparatus, which connected the arms of donor and recipient – was demonstrated in 1873.

bloodletting A medical procedure in which blood was withdrawn ('let') from the body by way of a vein or artery (general bloodletting) or through scarification, cupping or the application of leeches (local bloodletting). Though bloodletting can reduce congestion and vascular tension, it was a panacea popularly associated with the treatment of a number of minor ailments as well as more serious disorders such as pneumonia. Following controversy within the medical profession in the mid-1850s with regard to its efficacy the popularity of bloodletting declined among clinicians, though the practice retained some advocates among **physicians** well into the twentieth century.

Bloody Sunday On 13 November 1887 a demonstration in opposition to the government policy of **coercion** in Ireland was organised in Trafalgar Square, London, by the Metropolitan Radical Federation and the **Irish National League**. The 10,000 demonstrators were opposed by 2,000 police as well as 400 mounted Life Guards and foot soldiers from an infantry regiment. There were at least three fatalities, some 200 people were treated in hospital, and many more received injuries but were not hospitalised.

Bloomer costume An expression of a 'rational dress' movement opposed to the way in which female clothing inhibited personal movement and compromised hygiene, the Bloomer costume characteristically embodied a short jacket, a knee-length skirt, and a pair of ankle-length pantaloons which masked the contours of the wearer's exposed legs. Popularised – but not designed – by the American **temperance** enthusiast Amelia Jenks Bloomer (1818–94) in the 1850s, the costume was widely parodied in the popular press on both sides of the Atlantic, being associated with both female emancipation and the freedom of movement offered to women through access to the **bicycle**.

blue An undergraduate or graduate student of the University of Cambridge or the University of Oxford who has played in a competitive sport against the other institution – hence, a Victorian sportsman-scholar might 'win' a 'rowing blue' having competed in the **Boat Race**. The appellation recalls the shades of blue conventionally associated with the two ancient universities – dark for Oxford, light for Cambridge. The term has an occasional application, also, in the competitive sports played between **public schools**.

Boat Race A competitive and amateur sporting event between male scholars of the **universities** of Oxford and Cambridge, first run on 10 June 1829. The origins of the Boat Race lie in the **public school** system – the earliest challenge was issued by undergraduates who had joined their respective universities from Harrow and Eton – though for the first twenty-five years of its existence it was run as an irregular rather than annual competition. The Boat Race was to develop into both a public celebration of *mens sana in corpore sano* and a popular spectator event later in the century: the first equivalent boat race for women, however, was run only in 1927.

Boer A Dutch- or Afrikaans-speaking settler in British-ruled Southern Africa. The Boers were involved in pioneer farming in a wide region which embraced the Cape Colony, Transvaal, Orange Free State and Natal, their agricultural activities being inevitably associated with the colonial appropriation of land.

Boer Wars The British colonial administration in Southern Africa fought two wars against the **Boers** in 1880–81 (in the Transvaal) and 1899–1902 (across the Transvaal and in the Orange Free State). Both conflicts derived from British policies of expansionism – the Boers were active colonists, simultaneously appropriating African

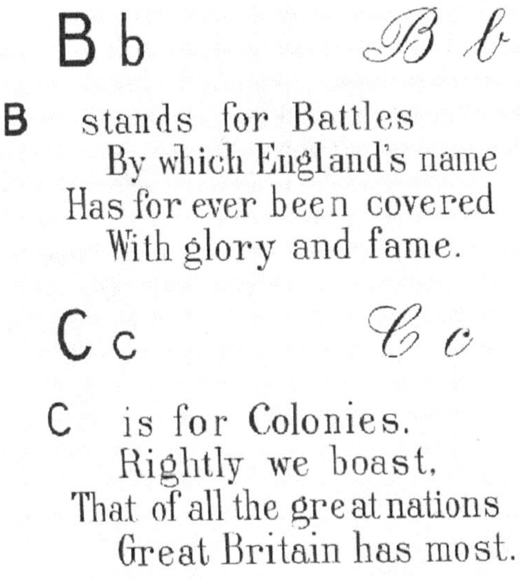

B b   *B b*

B   stands for Battles
       By which England's name
    Has for ever been covered
     With glory and fame.

C c   *C c*

C   is for Colonies.
       Rightly we boast,
    That of all the great nations
     Great Britain has most.

Figure 4 The British campaigns in South Africa provided a salutary reminder that continued military success and enduring colonial obedience could not be taken for granted. Caption from Mrs E. A. Ames, *ABC for Baby Patriots* (1899).

tribal lands and resisting any assertion of British influence over their new possessions – and were implicated not merely in the agricultural exploitation of the land but also in the extraction of diamonds from 1867. One important consequence of both conflicts was the realisation that the Boers' guerrilla tactics were more effective than the conventional strategy deployed by the British Army, and that the cumbersome weapons and brightly coloured uniforms of the latter often placed combatants at a disadvantage in South African terrain.

bombazine A dress material made of **worsted**, worsted combined with cotton, or worsted with silk. In black, bombazine was a popular material for formal **mourning**. See also: **crepe**.

Bond Street A fashionable commercial thoroughfare in London's West End which links Oxford Street and Piccadilly. Associated with luxury shopping, Bond Street incorporates the Royal **Arcade** (opened 1880) and was also the location of the **Grosvenor Gallery** (opened 1877).

Book of Common Prayer The 1662 *Book of Common Prayer* should be understood as representing far more than the duly authorised ceremonies of the **Anglican** church. In both its rejection of certain **Roman Catholic** rituals and in its incorporation of the statement of belief that is the **Thirty-Nine Articles** of Religion, the *Prayer Book* (as the volume is also commonly known) is an expression of the pervasive **Protestant** consciousness which arguably underwrites much of British domestic, as well as imperial, culture. 'The Table of Kindred and Affinity', which defines those persons who may not be married according to the rites of the Church of England, is also normally appended to the volume. A revised version of the *Prayer Book* was published for the Church of Ireland in 1878 following its **disestablishment** in 1871.

boots A low-ranking domestic or hotel **servant** – often a young boy – whose primary function was to clean the footwear of his employers or the hotel residents each evening.

bosjesman A derogative **Boer** expression applied to the aboriginal inhabitants of Southern Africa, considered to be 'bushmen' who dwell in the *bosje*, or uncultivated forest.

Botany Bay The site of the first British landing in New South Wales, Australia, in 1770, and a location popularly (though erroneously) associated with **transportation** in the nineteenth century. The first penal colony was at nearby Port Jackson.

Bow Street Runners A forerunner of the Metropolitan **Police** Force, established in 1749. See also: **Cato Street Conspiracy.**

boxing A regulated combative sport, descended from unregulated pugilism, practised by men across the whole spectrum of social class, and encouraged as an expression of the physical aspect of *mens sana in corpore sano* in the **public schools**, the army and navy. Prize-fighting, or bare-knuckle boxing, was historically a popular, if bloody, spectator sport as well as an important focus for gambling, frequently attracting the patronage of the sporting aristocracy. Increasingly regulated by custom and usage across the nineteenth century – the London Prize Ring Rules proving a particular reference point between the 1830s and 1850s – the conventions of amateur pugilism utilising padded gloves were codified most influentially in 1867 with the publication of a body of rules under the patronage of John Sholto Douglas (1844–1900), 9th Marquis of Queensbury.

box-wallah An Anglo-Indian term denoting a person who works in trade or commerce. See also: **wallah.**

boycott A withdrawal of social or financial contact with an organisation or individual, undertaken in order to protest, punish, exert pressure or achieve change. The term dates from 1880 and a campaign of isolation conducted against Charles Boycott (1832–97), land agent to Lord Erne (1802–85), by the **Irish National Land League.**

Boys' Brigade The first uniformed youth organisation, founded in Glasgow in 1883. Organised on military principles, the Boys' Brigade (BB) aimed to inculcate both Christian morals and manly standards of physicality through a form of **muscular Christianity.**

Boy's Own Paper, The Issued as a wholesome alternative to the **penny dreadfuls** by the **Religious Tract Society** from 1879, a weekly paper for boys which featured original and translated stories and topical articles.

Bradshaw's In full, *Bradshaw's Railway Guide*, a compendium of British railway timetables, first published in 1839. The Bradshaw name was also applied to a number of travel-related publications, including Continental and Imperial railway guides and the tourist-oriented 'Bradshaw's Tours' within *Bradshaw's Descriptive Railway Hand-Book of Great Britain and Ireland*. See also: **Baedeker.**

Figure 5 Cover of the first issue of *The Boy's Own Paper* (1879).

breeching The occasion when a small boy was first dressed in trousers (or breeches), rather than the short frock which both sexes wore in infancy. There was no specific age for breeching, and as a rite of passage its significance was perhaps confined to the middle and upper classes, where childhood extended over a longer period.

briar A **tobacco** pipe made of wood obtained from the root of a Mediterranean shrub. See also: **meerschaum**.

bride cake A rich fruit cake, shared at weddings.

bridewell A prison or **house of correction**.

bridge A card game for four players, which became a fixture in middle- and upper-class social intercourse later in the century. See also: **euchre; whist**.

Britannia The personification of Britain as a confident woman seated next to the sea, bearing a trident and a shield upon which the **Union Flag** is depicted. The image was a popular signifier of the British Empire as well as of the four nations of the United Kingdom, and appeared upon the penny, the basic unit of domestic **currency**. See also: **John Bull**.

Figure 6 Reverse ('tail') side of a penny coin showing Britannia (1887).

Britannia metal An alloy of tin, antimony and copper, resembling silver and used in the manufacture of cheap tableware.

British and Foreign Bible Society Founded in 1804 by the anti-slavery campaigner William Wilberforce (1759–1833) and members of the **Clapham Sect**, an organisation which distributed Christian bibles in the English language and funded their translation into other languages. See also: **Religious Tract Society**.

British Israelism A minor and largely **Protestant** movement, growing in popularity from the 1880s, which believed that the ostensibly indigenous peoples of the British Isles were the descendants of the ten 'lost' (or resettled) tribes of Israel. A belief in the biblical origin of the British nation imbricates theology and politics: the Jews, as God's chosen people (Deut. 14:2), are presumed to enjoy an implicit destiny as well as a divine antiquity.

broad church That part of the **Anglican** Church which believes that the denomination should be comprehensive and tolerant in matters of belief and ritual. See also: **evangelical; high church**.

broadcloth Fabric for clothing, woven to a greater width than ordinary cloth.

brummagem Counterfeit or sham goods, or a cheap imitation of a better-quality article.

Buckingham Palace The official London residence of the Sovereign from 1837. Prior to the accession of Queen Victoria, the monarch resided at St James's Palace.

Bulgarian Horrors So named by the **Liberal** statesman William Ewart Gladstone (1809–98), a series of reprisals carried out by Ottoman forces in order to repress the 1876 Bulgarian uprising. The so-called Eastern Question of 1875–8 drew the attention of the British public to the presence of Turkey in Europe, and in particular of the difficult situation faced by European Christians under nominal Islamic rule. Gladstone's open sympathy for the Bulgarians notably contrasted the **Conservative** policy of Benjamin Disraeli (1804–81), which maintained a tacit support for Turkey as a political counterweight to Russian ambitions in the Balkans. The Eastern Question was ostensibly concluded by the Congress of Berlin in 1878, which created an autonomous province of Bulgaria under Ottoman sovereignty. See also: **bashi-bazouks**.

burial club A financial scheme, sometimes organised by a church or **friendly society**, to which an individual subscribed in order to fund their own funeral or pay for that that of another family member.

burra peg See: **chota peg**.

bustle A padded wire or wooden frame, worn beneath a woman's skirt. Particularly fashionable in the 1870s and 1880s, bustles accentuated the hips and the posterior, the rigid frame occasionally being replaced by fabric padding or collapsible structures.

butcher boots A riding boot which extends to just below the knee. Unlike **top boots**, butcher boots do not feature a contrasting panel or cuff immediately below the knee: in **hunting**, butcher boots are correctly worn with a black – rather than scarlet or **hunting pink** – coat.

butler The most senior male **servant** in a household. The butler was responsible for the custody of the household's silverware and wine cellar, maintained discipline and decorum over the servants, and supervised the serving of meals and the care of guests.

button hook An implement featuring a hook or loop, used to fasten the buttons which closed ankle boots and **spats**.

bwana A Swahili word meaning 'master', used as a conventional and respectful form of address towards Europeans by colonial subjects.

| C |

calabash A type of **tobacco** pipe, made either from, or else shaped to resemble, a calabash gourd.

calico A variety of printed or plain cotton cloth, originally imported from India.

calling card A printed card, bearing the owner's name and address. The function of the calling card is somewhat different from that of the modern business card in that it signifies the presence of its owner rather than merely conveying information about them. Hence, the card would be conveyed to the householder by a domestic **servant** to formally announce the arrival of a visitor, or else left at the door if a visit could not be paid in person. Also known as a visiting card or, when a photograph is incorporated, a **carte de visite**.

cannabis Introduced from India as a novel medical remedy from 1841, cannabis tincture was deployed as an analgesic for menstrual disorders and as a suppressant in convulsions and spasmodic disorders. Though often prescribed by medical practitioners, it never achieved the popularity of **opium**-based preparations such as **black drop**, and was rarely smoked as a recreational drug outside of Asia in the nineteenth century.

canon In **Anglican** use, a clergyman associated with the management of a cathedral or abbey. Also known as a prebendary.

canon law The body of legislation through which the **Anglican** Church is administered. See also: **Doctors' Commons**.

capital punishment The death penalty could, in theory, be imposed for a wide variety of offences against property and the person across the first four decades of the century. Numerous pieces of legislation enacted between 1823 and 1841 progressively reduced the number of these, so that between 1836 and 1841 executions were only administered in respect of individuals convicted for murder or attempted murder. After 1841, murder was effectively the only capital offence for which a sentence of execution was routinely pronounced, though the law retained the penalty for those convicted of treason, piracy and arson in a royal dockyard. At the discretion of the presiding judge, a sentence of death might be pronounced but with a formal recommendation of mercy which would commute the sentence to transportation or imprisonment. See also: **public execution**.

carbuncle A red-coloured precious stone. The term is also applied medically to pustules or boils on the skin, particularly when these are red or inflamed.

card case A small container, often metallic, in which **calling cards** are carried.

card games See: baccarat; bridge; chemin de fer; euchre; whist.

Carlton Club Founded in London in 1832, an elite gentlemen's club closely associated with the development of the modern **Conservative Party**. Women were not admitted to the club as full members until 2008.

Carnegie libraries A series of local, independent and free public libraries founded and partially funded by Andrew Carnegie (1835–1919), a Scottish-born American industrialist. The first library opened in the donor's birthplace, Dunfermline, in 1883, and while Carnegie funded similar institutions globally, his earliest philanthropic activities in Victorian Britain prioritised Scottish towns and cities.

carte de visite A small photographic print, popular from 1854. Though these pictures were sometimes deployed as **calling cards**, cartes de visite which depicted celebrities or royalty were widely collected and traded.

Catholic Association An organisation, established in 1823 by the Irish politician Daniel O'Connell (1775–1847), which campaigned for **Catholic Emancipation**.

Catholic Emancipation The 1829 *Act for the Relief of His Majesty's Roman Catholic Subjects* (10 Geo. 4 c. 7) permitted **Roman Catholics** to be elected as Members of Parliament, thus repealing their disqualification under several laws enacted in the seventeenth and eighteenth centuries. The passing of the act arguably demonstrated the possibility that further reform of the franchise might be achieved, with disqualification on account of wealth rather than because of religion becoming the focus of subsequent agitation.

Catholic Truth Society A publishing and evangelising organisation, founded in 1868, which aimed to communicate the doctrines, and enhance the public presence, of the **Roman Catholic** Church in Britain. See also: **Protestant Alliance**.

Catholic University of Ireland A private **Roman Catholic** university, founded in Dublin in 1851 as a reaction to the establishment of the non-denominational **Queen's University of Ireland**. The first Rector was a former **Anglican**, John Henry Newman (1801–90). See also: **Royal University of Ireland; universities**.

Cato Street Conspiracy A plot which aimed to murder the **Tory** prime minister Robert Banks Jenkinson (1770–1828) and his ministerial colleagues in 1820. The revolutionary group behind the plot, known as the Spencean Philanthropists, had been infiltrated by a government agent and the conspirators were apprehended by the **Bow Street Runners**, one of whom was killed in the encounter. Five of the conspirators were publicly hanged and posthumously beheaded for treason; five others were sentenced to **transportation** for life.

Cetewayo One of several variant spellings – others include Cetywayo and Cetshwayo – of the name of the **Zulu** king Cetshwayo kaMpande (1826–84), who reigned between 1873 and 1879.

Ceylon [Sri Lanka] Captured from the Dutch by the **East India Company** in 1796, a strategically important island off the south-eastern coast of India. British political control was established in 1815, and agriculture – based upon **indentured labour** brought from the Subcontinent – was developed, first around coffee and later tea, rubber and coconuts.

chai-wallah An Anglo-Indian term denoting a vendor of hot tea, particularly to travellers temporarily halted at **railway** stations, army camps and **dâk** bungalows. The spelling is sometimes rendered as char-wallah.

Chancery The court of the Lord Chancellor of England, and second only to the **House of Lords**. One of its two tribunals was concerned with the issuing of writs for each new parliament. The other – which was often the subject of published satire ridiculing the slowness and expense of its proceedings – was a court of equity or common law in which appeals might be heard.

chapel Colloquially, a place of **Roman Catholic** or **Protestant** worship which is not associated with the **Anglican** church. See also: **conventicle**.

chapel of ease In **Anglican** usage, an additional place of worship built within a large **parish** for the convenience of worshippers who dwell some distance from the parish church.

charabanc A horse-drawn, and usually open-topped, vehicle in which a large number of seated passengers might be conveyed. See also: **omnibus**.

Charge of the Light Brigade A disastrous military action undertaken by British light cavalry during the Battle of Balaclava – an engagement in the **Crimean War** – on 25 October 1854. Deficient lines of communication between senior British officers led to the cavalry being cut down by Russian forces on three sides of a valley during the charge.

charpoy A lightly constructed bed, as used in India.

charter In **university** usage, a document issued either by the Crown or by Parliament which formally establishes or recognises an educational institution, and thus implicitly confers upon it the right to award qualifications under its own name and title.

Chartism A popular movement agitating for an extension of the franchise to working-class men between 1836 and 1848. It proposed a People's Charter of six points, these being: a vote for all men over the age of twenty-one years; a secret, rather than public, ballot; the removal of the requirement for Members of Parliament to be property holders; the payment of Members of Parliament for their services; electoral districts of equal size; and annual elections for Parliament. Petitions to this effect were presented to Parliament in 1839, 1842 and 1848, and all were rejected. Though largely a reform movement premised upon peaceful protest or 'moral force', 'physical force' Chartism was associated with rioting in Newport, South Wales, in 1839, where twenty-two protestors were shot by troops, and in Preston in 1842.

chemin de fer A version of the card game **baccarat**, associated with gambling and gaining wide notoriety following a cheating scandal in 1890 – the Tranby Croft affair – which led to the appearance of the **Prince of Wales** in court as a witness in 1891.

cheroot A small and slender cigar, originally manufactured in India, with a relatively strong taste for its size. See also: **smoking**.

Chiltern Hundreds Under a resolution enacted as early as 1624, a Member of Parliament (MP) cannot directly resign a seat in the **House of Commons** during the lifetime of a parliament, but has instead to apply for a nominal public office which cannot be occupied by a sitting MP. The two offices customarily recognised for this purpose are those of 'Crown Steward' and 'Bailiff of the Chiltern Hundreds and of the Manor of Northstead': individuals who apply for these posts are considered 'disqualified', and their parliamentary seats rendered subject to a by-election. Other than disqualification, a parliamentary seat may only be vacated by the death of the member or his formal expulsion from the House.

Chlorodyne An **opium**-infused **patent medicine**, invented as an antidote for **cholera** in 1857 by John Collis Browne (1819–84), and
later marketed under several brand names as a cure for asthma,
bronchitis, **consumption**, coughs and **hysteria**.

Chloroform A colourless liquid which, when inhaled, produces insen-
sibility. Discovered in 1831, it was used in chemical **anaesthesia**
from 1847.

cholera An often fatal disease, the symptoms of which include vertigo,
nausea, vomiting, heavy perspiration, stomach cramps, and the
passing of stools which resemble rice water. There were serious
cholera **epidemics** in Britain in 1831–2, 1848–9, 1853–4 and
1855–6, the disease in each case having spread along international trade routes. John Snow (1813–58), a **physician** in **Soho**,
established as early as 1849 that cholera was transmitted by
contaminated water rather than as an airborne miasma, though
his conclusions only gained substantial acceptance following his
intervention in the 1854 Soho outbreak.

chophouse An eating house, often cheap rather than exclusive, where
dishes such as mutton chops are served.

Figure 7 Cholera, like typhus, is spread through contaminated drinking
water. George Pinwell, 'Death's Dispensary', *Fun*, 18 August 1866.

chota peg A colonial term for a small measure of spirits, often, whisky or gin. A burra peg was a large measure, *burra* and *chota* being, apparently, adjectives of Hindi origin.

Christian Socialism A reformist movement advocating a version of socialism conducted according to Christian principles which emerged following the failure of **Chartism**. The term was coined by the **Anglican** clergyman Frederick Denison Maurice (1805–72) in 1848, and the movement's political influences derive more from cultural **Romanticism**, tempered by the philosophy of Thomas Carlyle (1795–1881) than the political theory of Karl Marx (1818–83). Under the loose leadership of educated and largely middle-class thinkers and writers, Christian Socialism was advertised to the working classes by way of pamphlets and proclamations and through the encouragement of profit-sharing enterprises such as the **co-operative movement**. Beyond economics, the tenets of Christian Socialism were closely associated with those of **muscular Christianity**, and the movement influenced, among others, the novelist Thomas Hughes (1822–96) and the **broad church** cleric Charles Kingsley (1819–75).

Christmas While not designated a **bank holiday** by law in the nineteenth century, 25 December was customarily observed as a day of rest from commercial activity across much of the country. Though Prince Albert has conventionally been credited with the introduction of the Christmas tree to British culture, Queen Charlotte (1744–1818), the German wife of George III (1738–1820), is reputed to have displayed one as early as 1800.

chukka The discrete periods into which play is divided during a **polo** match.

Church Army An **Anglican** organisation, established in 1882, and deploying a structure reminiscent of the earlier **Salvation Army**. The organisation opened colleges to train male and female missionaries to work in British cities, conducted **evangelical** work in prisons, and funded horse-drawn mission caravans which travelled from town to town.

Church of England See: **Anglican**.

Church of Scotland Popularly known as the **Kirk**, a Presbyterian (rather than Episcopalian) **Protestant** denomination which in Scotland fulfils many of the ecclesiastical and ceremonial functions associated with the **Anglican** Church in England.

cigarette Originally a hand-rolled paper tube containing little more than the discarded and fragmentary sweepings from the production of more expensive cigars or pipe tobacco, the mass-produced cigarette became subject to viable production following the invention of the Bonsack machine in 1880. Introduced into Britain in 1883, automation led to the development of large commercial cigarette factories in seaports such as Bristol, Liverpool and Belfast, and an enhanced popularity for the cigarette as a cheap recreational distraction – convenient, quickly consumed – and still sufficiently radical as to be attractive to the iconoclastic **New Woman**.

circulating libraries Commercial libraries, from which middle-class subscribers might borrow and return books either in person or through the postal system. Library proprietors exercised great influence over both writing and publishing, policing the morality of publications and dictating the division of novels into a **triple-decker** (three-volume) format in order to encourage the purchase of further subscriptions. Mudie's Select Library (1840–1937) was the best known of the circulating libraries, while W. H. Smith's (1860–1961) distributed books through its commercial outlets in **railway** stations. Working-class library provision was limited for much of the century to the largely practical works held by mechanics' institutes. Broader public collections were initiated through the philanthropy of Andrew **Carnegie** (1835–1919), who established free public libraries in Britain from 1883.

circumcision The removal of the foreskin either as a religious rite de passage, or as a medical procedure to deter a young boy from the ostensibly pernicious habit of **onanism**.

Clapham Sect A group of wealthy **evangelical Protestants**, active between 1790 and 1830 in Clapham, London, who were involved in the campaign against **slavery**, the **British and Foreign Bible Society**, and the promotion of human and animal wellbeing.

clasp knife A pocket knife constructed so that the blade folds back into the handle when not in use.

Cleveland Street Scandal The discovery of a **house of assignation** on the road which divides Westminster from Camden by London **police** in 1889 led to scandalous newspaper reportage which, while reporting accurately with regard to the employment of young Post Office workers as male prostitutes, speculated wildly that the brothel's **homosexual** and bisexual habitués included noblemen and, possibly, royalty.

clipper A fast sailing vessel, often associated with the mid-century transport of **tea** from China to England but also active on transatlantic sea routes, particularly during the gold rushes in California (1848) and Australia (1851). The popularity of clippers declined with the opening of the **Suez Canal** in 1869 and the development of reliable steam technology.

clubs Predominantly organised on a financially exclusive and single-sex basis, clubs provided a discreet social space in which gentlemen could meet, dine, transact business privately and, in some cases, avail themselves of overnight accommodation on the premises. In many cases, reciprocal agreements permitted the members of one club to use some or all of the facilities of another when travelling, thus maintaining a network which facilitated business across the Empire. Club facilities would characteristically include a library which received the national as well as local newspapers, a dining room and separate bar (within which guests might be received), rooms for **billiards, snooker** and **smoking,** and a confidential concierge service which could receive and deliver communications as well as forming a polite barrier against non-members. The customary exclusion of women from the London clubs located in **St James's** prompted the formation of corresponding single-sex meeting places for educated women in particular: the Somerville Club, for members of the Oxford **University** College of the same name, was founded in 1879; the University Club (founded 1887) drew its members from **Somerville College** or **Lady Margaret Hall**, Oxford and from **Newnham** or **Girton College**, Cambridge. The Alexandra Club (founded 1884) restricted its membership to women eligible to attend Court – that is, to be in the company of the monarch. Clubs in the British Empire tended to be more relaxed with regard to gender exclusivity, some incorporating a 'mixed bar' as well as discrete ladies' and gentlemen's bars. Racial segregation remained, however, the norm well into the twentieth century, and many clubs did not admit non-Europeans. See also: **Athenaeum Club; Carlton Club; Reform Club.**

coal gas Flammable gas, derived from heated coal, was used in street lamps as early as 1812 and, more rarely, for cooking from the 1840s. Though factories and public buildings were often lit by gas by the 1850s, domestic gas illumination was largely confined to wealthier houses until the last quarter of the century.

coal owner The proprietor of a coal mine.

cobblestones Naturally rounded pieces of hardwearing stone (sometimes called cobbles), laid down as the surface of a road or path. See also: **sett**.

Cockney Strictly speaking, an individual born within the sound of the bells of St Mary-le-Bow Church, London, but more colloquially a Londoner, particularly a working-class inhabitant of the East End. See also: **'Arry and 'Arriet**.

Coercion Acts A term which covers a number of governmental measures applied to Ireland between 1833 and 1887 which at different times facilitated curfews (1833, 1847), suspended **habeas corpus** (1871, 1881), permitted trials for certain offences under three judges and created a legal offence of intimidation (1882).

coke hat Pronounced 'cook', the original name for the bowler (or derby) hat, commissioned for the gamekeepers of Holkham Hall, Norfolk, in 1849.

Commissioners' Gothic A style of **Gothic Revival architecture** approved for the construction of **Anglican** churches under the *Church Building Act* (58 Geo. 3 c. 45) of 1818 and subsequent legislation.

confinement See: **accouchement**.

consent, age of Distinct from the age of **majority**, this is the point at which an individual is deemed sufficiently responsible to consent to sexual intercourse. Under the 1861 *Offences Against the Person Act* (**24 & 25 Vict. c. 100**), the age of consent for heterosexual congress was 12; it was raised to 16 by the 1885 *Criminal Law Amendment Act* (**48 & 49 Vict. c. 69**). This latter legislation also enhanced the existing criminalisation of **homosexuality**. See also: **Labouchère Amendment**.

Conservative Party Formally established as such in the 1830s, but popularly retaining the name of an earlier 'Tory' political identity, the earliest policies of the party were set out by Robert Peel (1788–1850) in the **Tamworth Manifesto** of 1834. Broadly, the party supported manufacturing and commercial as well as landed interests across the nineteenth century, made much of its commitment to law, order and civil stability, and tended towards a broadly **Protestant**, and sometimes specifically **Anglican**, conception of national identity. The party survived schism over the **Corn Laws** in 1846, and later in the century attracted dissidents from its only realistic political opponent outside of Ireland, the **Liberal Party,** when the latter became divided over Irish **Home Rule.**

consumption The popular name for **tuberculosis** or **phthisis,** a drop-let-transmitted disease of the lungs, which was at best debilita-tive, and at worst fatal, to those who contracted it.

Contagious Diseases Acts See: venereal disease.

conventicle A meeting of **dissenters,** or the building in which a **Protestant** (but *not* **Anglican**) act of worship might be held. See also: **chapel.**

coolie Colloquially, an unskilled or **indentured labourer** employed on a plantation, as a porter or carrier, or as a railway or construc-tion worker. The term has derogatory and racist implications.

co-operative movement Drawing upon the ideas of Robert Owen (1771–1858), a mutually beneficial and trading organisation founded in Lancashire in 1844 by the **Rochdale Pioneers.** The earliest co-operative store sold only basic foodstuffs and candles, but without **adulteration** and with a discount that priced them favourably when compared to goods sold through the **truck sys-tem.** The number of co-operative shops expanded across the cen-tury as other local societies developed on the Rochdale model, and a wholesale arm was established in 1863 which extended activities into farming, manufacturing and importing.

copper A slang term for a small-denomination coin, originally minted in copper, such as a **farthing,** halfpenny or penny. Also a slang term for a **police** officer. See also: **currency.**

Corn Laws Protectionist legislation first enacted in 1815 which restricted the import of cheap wheat in order to maintain the price (and profitability) of domestic supplies. Inimical with the doctrine of **Free Trade,** and disproportionate in their effect upon the low paid, they were repealed under Robert Peel (1788–1850) in 1846.

cornet A commissioned officer in a cavalry regiment with responsibility for the regiment's standards or 'colours'. The title was abolished in 1870, though it survived in popular usage and as an internal distinction within certain mounted regiments,

Cornhill Magazine A monthly magazine, founded in 1860, which special-ised in fiction, poetry and literary essays by prominent authors such as Wilkie Collins (1824–89), George Eliot (1819–80), Elizabeth Gaskell (1810–65) and Alfred, Lord Tennyson (1809–92).

corset A female undergarment, fastened with laces and stiffened with wood, whalebone or steel, which enhances the shape of the body by compressing the waistline.

coursing See: hare coursing.

crape See: crepe.

cremation An ostensibly hygienic mode of disposing of human remains, cremation became topical as cemeteries became overcrowded with interments, and the cost of elaborate **funerals** increased. The Cremation Society, which advanced arguments with regard to both the advantages and the legality of the process, was founded in 1874, and constructed the first practical crematorium in Woking in 1879: this facility was not used until 1885, cremation having been deemed legal only in 1884.

crepe Sometimes spelled 'crape', a thin and plain material which, when dyed black, was regarded as the most suitable fabric for garments worn to signify **mourning**.

cricket Codified from 1744, the laws (rather than 'rules') of cricket were revised in 1835 and 1884, with the Marylebone Cricket Club, or MCC (founded 1787), acting as custodian of the game. County cricket was supported by the MCC from 1870, and the first tour of Australia took place in 1877. This latter event arguably crystallises the function of cricket in enhancing a common sporting culture for the British Empire, as well as county and regional identities in those places where the game was, and is, played.

crim. con. The abbreviated form of 'criminal conversation', a legal term which denotes **adultery**, and is deployed in legal actions which may lead to **divorce**. Crim. con. was abolished as a specific crime by the 1857 *Matrimonial Causes Act* (<u>20 & 21 Vict. c. 85</u>), though the offended husband remained legally able to claim financial compensation from his male counterpart.

Crimean War A military conflict, fought 1853–6, between Russia and an alliance of Britain, France, the Ottoman Empire and Sardinia. The war was fought using the modern weaponry of **shrapnel shells** and steam-powered battleships, and the communicative technology of **railways** and **telegraphy**, though harsh winter conditions, disease and injuries highlighted the deficiency of care customarily exercised by the army over the troops. Graphic newspaper reportage contributed to the unpopularity of the conflict in Britain, and added impetus to the professionalising of supporting agencies such as medical services. See also: **Charge of the Light Brigade**.

Crockford's In full, *Crockford's Clerical Directory*, this now biennial publication was initially advertised as 'a biographical and statistical book of reference for facts relating to the clergy and the church'. First published in 1858 by John Crockford (c.1823–65) possibly in association with Edward Cox (1809–79), publisher of the *Law Times*, it was concerned solely with the **Anglican** Church.

croquet A genteel lawn game in which wooden balls are directed through a series of iron arches by means of a wooden mallet. Formal rules for the game were laid down in 1856, and a Croquet Association founded in 1897.

Figure 8 Thomas Crane, 'The Crossing Sweeper' from Thomas Crane and Ellen Houghton, *London Town* (1883).

crossing sweeper An individual, frequently an elderly semi-vagrant or younger **street Arab**, who solicits payment for clearing urban roads of offensive refuse, such as horse manure, so that genteel travellers may pass without soiling their shoes or lower garments.

Crown Steward See: **Chiltern Hundreds.**

Crystal Palace The cast-iron and glass modular accommodation designed by Joseph Paxton (1803–65) for the 1851 **Great Exhibition.**

cupping See: **bloodletting.**

curate A junior clergyman who assists the incumbent minister of an Anglican **parish.**

currency Prior to decimalisation in 1971, British currency was reckoned in pounds, **shillings** and pence. The pound was made up of 240 pence, or pennies; the shilling was worth twelve pence; and the penny might be further divided into two halfpence (known colloquially as ha'pennies) or four farthings. In written form, the sum of 2 pounds, 3 shillings and sixpence would conventionally appear as either '£2 3s 6d.' or '£2 3/6'; three shillings alone would be written as '3/-'. The abbreviation 'd.' is derived from the Latin 'denarius', and occasionally the letter 'L' (for 'libra') might be found in place of the symbol '£'. See also: **guinea.**

D

dacoit A class of robber, usually a member of a group, and active in the area between Burma (now Myanmar) and India.

daguerreotype An type of early photograph, developed from 1839.

dâk Sometimes spelled 'dawk', a route or relay system for travellers in India, with overnight accommodation provided at dâk bungalows.

dâk-wallah A letter-carrier in British India.

dark lantern A portable lantern fitted with a shutter which, when closed, conceals the light.

dawk See: **dâk.**

Debrett's In full, *Debrett's Peerage, Baronetage and Knightage*, a reference work which provides information upon the titled families of the United Kingdom in addition to the appropriate titles of courtesy and modes of address that should be observed in communication with the nobility. The publication can trace its origins to 1769, and the name of the publisher and bookseller John Debrett (1753–1822) became part of the title in 1802. The Debrett name became further associated with manuals of etiquette in the twentieth century. See also: **baronet.**

debtors' prison Until 1869, debtors could be imprisoned indefinitely for insolvency, release being conditional upon the discharge of the debt. The main prisons to which London debtors were routinely sent were the **Fleet** and **Marshalsea** (both closed in 1842), Farringdon (closed 1846), Whitecross Street (closed 1870) and King's Bench (closed 1880). Bankruptcies were publicly announced in the *London Gazette*.

debutante A young woman entering public life for the first time, usually by participating in one or more of the social events which make up the fashionable calendar of the **London season**.

decadence Associated with **Aestheticism** and the artistic temperament of the **fin de siècle**, a perception that culture – and possibly physicality also – had entered into **degeneration**, and that progress and improvement were no longer inevitable. The most prominent writer on the topic was Max Nordau (1849–1923), who perceived decadence in **Pre-Raphaelitism**, the stylish dandyism of Oscar Wilde, and the **opera** of Richard Wagner (1813–83).

deer stalking An elite **field sport** in which wild deer are stealthily followed ('stalked') at a distance by one or two hunters ('stalkers') armed with rifles.

deerstalker A hat, often of tweed or other thorn-proof cloth, and usually featuring adjustable ear flaps that may be tied above the head.

degeneration Conceptually related to the debate around **decadence**, a largely **fin de siècle** belief that the physicality of the nation is perceptibly deteriorating due to, variously, sexual immorality and **homosexuality**, freely available intoxicants such as alcohol or drugs, immigration and cultural contact with supposed colonial or 'foreign' vices, or environmental factors associated with urban living and the **adulteration** of foodstuffs. The central theorists of degeneration were Cesare Lombroso (1835–1909) and Edwin Ray Lankester (1847–1929). See also: **absinthe**.

Derby, the A celebrated English horse race – formally known as 'The Derby Stakes' – which has been run over a flat course on the Epsom Downs since 1780. 'Derby Day' is distinguished not merely by the race itself but also by the extensive social gathering which surrounds it. See also: **Grand National, the; steeplechase**.

dhobi-wallah A laundryman in India. Dhobi itch is a skin irritation of the groin.

dhow A single-masted sailing vessel, commonly used on the Arabian Sea.

disestablishment The legal procedure by which the **Anglican** Church was formally removed as the state church in Ireland (1871) and Wales (1914).

dissenters Also known as Nonconformists, the term describes members of **Protestant** denominations which do not recognise the doctrinal authority of the **Anglican** Church, and which are administratively and financially separate from it. The term is not customarily applied to members of the **Roman Catholic Church**.

divorce Before the mid-nineteenth century the primary method of obtaining a divorce was by way of a private Act of Parliament, **adultery** being the central ground for petition. The process was expensive and, furthermore, disadvantageous to female petitioners, who were required to prove life-threatening cruelty in addition to adultery on the part of the husband. In 1853 a Royal Commission recommended that the process be transferred from Parliament to the court system, and the 1857 *Matrimonial Causes Act* (**20 & 21 Vict. c. 85**) retained the earlier double standard by requiring the wife to state a compounding offence such as bigamy, cruelty, desertion or incest. Divorce, whether enacted before or after the 1857 Act, had serious implications for the financial situations of both partners, with the control of property and wealth often being subject to separate (and expensive) legal actions. The *Married Women's Property Act* of 1870 (**33 & 34 Vict. c. 93**), its amendment in 1874 and the *Married Women's Property Act* of 1882 (**45 & 46 Vict. c. 75**) must therefore be understood as being relevant to this issue.

Doctors' Commons A college or society of legal professionals, based in London, and involved with the administration of the **canon law** of the **Anglican** Church and the Court of Admiralty. The society was dissolved in 1858.

dog cart An open horse-drawn carriage with seats placed back to back, so that any passengers seated behind the driver would face away from the direction of travel. The term is derived from an earlier type of vehicle in which the rear-facing seats were placed above a box intended to carry the dogs which a **gun** would typically use to retrieve game during a grouse or **pheasant shoot**. Small carriages literally drawn by dogs, often intended for the entertainment of children, were not unknown in the nineteenth century, though the practice was made illegal under the 1854 *Cruelty to Animals Act* (17 & 18 Vict. c. 60).

domestic fiction Popular fiction, the events of which take place within the home, primarily marketed to female readers. Domestic fiction was readily adopted by Christian publishers such as the **Religious Tract Society** to demonstrate wholesome modes of behaviour to wives and mothers, as well as to convey moral and evangelical teaching. Rosa Nouchette Carey (1840–1909) was one of the most prolific, as well as the most popular, of authors in this tradition.

domestic sphere One of half of a popular dichotomy that divides social existence into a domestic world under delegated female governance – the home, as well as those whose existence is conducted primarily in that environment, such as children or servants – and the public sphere of business, commercial and financial life, which is assumed to be a male preserve. Though persistent and pervasive, this division must be treated with caution, as its demarcations often do not adequately account for working-class women in the workplace or the presence of otherwise unemployed men in the home, nor indeed to the changes in ownership and proprietorship associated with the *Married Women's Property Acts* of 1870 (**33 & 34 Vict. c. 93**) and 1882 (45 & 46 Vict. c. 75).

dosshouse A cheap lodging house, usually accommodating a number of people in a room rather than providing separate accommodation for individuals. Though a rudimentary bed might be provided, some establishments provided only a seat for the night, and daytime accommodation on the premises was seldom available. Better-quality establishments of this type were managed by organisations such as the **Salvation Army**, as much for the long-term **evangelical** possibilities they presented as for the temporary relief of poverty and homelessness.

drag A private carriage, similar to a **stagecoach**, which is drawn by four horses.

dray A low, horse-drawn vehicle, particularly associated with the transport of beer.

dry bob See: **wet bob**.

drysalter A dealer in chemical products, such as dyes, oils and certain legal drugs. Drysalters might also sell preserved foodstuffs such as pickles or sauces.

Dublin Review, The A **Roman Catholic** periodical, published in London from 1836, and marketed to both educated members of that Church and to **Protestants** interested in contemporary Catholic thought. The periodical influenced members of the **Oxford Movement**, and **Tractarian** converts were among its later contributors.

duelling Because of its ambiguous legality, and the abiding tradition which understands that matters of honour must be settled in the company of but one or two supporters (or 'seconds'), the actual extent of duelling in the nineteenth century is far from clear. Some duels, certainly, appear to have been conducted symbolically, if not ceremonially, with no intent to wound or kill on either side, though the practice seems to have had sufficient reality for it to be condemned in a speech reported in *Hansard* on 14 March 1844. The last recorded duel fought on British soil occurred reputedly near Windsor in 1852, both combatants being French nationals.

dumb waiter Either a piece of furniture used to convey or store dishes and food within a dining room, or else a boxlike elevator used to convey the same from a basement kitchen to a dining area situated on one of the floors above.

Dundrearies Also known as Piccadilly weepers, these were affectedly long and drooping sideburns which enjoyed a fashionable vogue in the last quarter of the nineteenth century despite their original association with the foppish aristocratic figure of Lord Dundreary in the play *Our American Cousin* (1858) by Tom Taylor (1817–80). Dundrearyisms – derived from the speech of Taylor's fictional aristocrat – are distorted versions of familiar phrases, particularly where two different figures of speech are run together.

dunn A term used to describe both a creditor who presses for the repayment of money which is owing, or, alternatively, a debt collector or an agent employed by such a creditor.

dust A Victorian euphemism for mixed household waste, including food scraps and (often) human excrement. Collected by commercial dust-men, the dust was sold on for use as fertiliser, as an additive for brick-making, and – when sorted from the dust-heap – in the form of scrap metal and other reusable products. See also: **night-soil man**.

dyspepsia A disorder of the digestive system, often associated with overindulgence.

E

ear trumpet A small conical device, the narrower end of which is held to the ear in order to magnify speech and other sounds.

East India Company A **joint-stock company** founded in 1600 to initiate and exploit a formally sanctioned monopoly of trade between England, eastern Asia and India. The commercial aims of the Company were imbricated with both the domestic politics and imperial aspirations of England (and, later, Britain), and it became actively involved in **slavery**, the **tea** trade, and the export of **opium** to China. In nineteenth-century India, the Company remained responsible for the garrisoning and administration of the various territories into which its influence extended until the **Indian Mutiny** of 1857, the subsequent *Government of India Act* (21 & 22 Vict. c. 106) stating that 'India shall be governed by, and in the name of, Her Majesty'. See also: **Opium Wars**.

East India Pale Ale See: **India Pale Ale**.

Eglinton tournament An imaginative recreation of a mediaeval tournament, in which a core body of twelve knights – all of them members of the nobility or gentry – jousted and paraded in front of an audience that included members of both the **Tory** aristocracy and the general public at Eglinton Castle, North Ayrshire, Scotland. The tournament opened on 28 August 1839 and was ignominiously disrupted by heavy rain. Though the jousting was resumed on 30 August, the day's mêlées being followed by a banquet and ball for which invited guests donned medieval costume, the tournament became the subject of satire in both **Whig** and radical periodicals. The significance of the event, though, was in its popularising of a chivalric and medieval ideal, variously nostalgic and idealised, which was to influence gendered behaviour generally, and the education of gentlemen through vigorous *mens sana in corpore sano* specifically.

eisteddfod A significant component of the development of a resurgent Welsh cultural tradition in the early nineteenth century, eisteddfodau (the plural) facilitated the revival of traditional forms of Welsh-language verse and distinctive music across the Principality. These artistic activities, in turn, arguably stimulated a nascent nationalism based upon cultural and linguistic difference. A National Eisteddfod Association was formed in Wales in 1880, though eisteddfodau were held outside of the Principality from the late nineteenth century – for example in the Welsh-speaking colony of Y Wladfa in Patagonia (founded 1865) in 1880 and in Liverpool in 1884 and 1900.

electricity More expensive to produce and distribute than **coal gas**, electricity was not widely exploited for lighting purposes until the twentieth century. Domestic filament bulbs were available in Britain from the 1870s, and a trial of electric arc street lighting was initiated in Edinburgh as early as 1881. It was on the **railways**, though, that electricity was to be extensively developed both as a non-polluting source of motive power, ideally adapted to underground and elevated mass-transit systems, and to the illumination of carriages, tunnels and signalling systems. The first electric passenger line, Volk's Electric Railway, opened as a tourist attraction in Brighton in 1883, electricity was introduced on London's **underground railways** in 1890, and in 1893 an electrified overhead railway was opened in Liverpool: commercial investment favoured relatively short lines rather than intercity networks.

elementary education Also known as primary education, a basic level of literacy and mathematical knowledge – colloquially the 'three Rs' of reading, writing and arithmetic – often accompanied by moral or religious training, pursued by younger children. In Victorian Britain, this training might be provided through religious or secular institutions, though state intervention was enhanced by way of a series of Elementary Education Acts in 1870 (**Forster's Education Act**), 1876 and 1891.

enceinte Adopted from the French, a polite euphemism for pregnancy.

Enquire Within upon Everything A series of cheap self-help books, first marketed in 1856 and regularly revised and republished thereafter, which instructed a primarily working-class readership in topics as various as making a will, arranging a funeral, or hosting a dinner party.

entail A legal action by which the right to inherit property or the ownership of an estate might be limited to certain descendants, in order to ensure that it is not divided or does not pass out of family ownership.

entire A type of commercially brewed beer which combined the lighter flavours of fresh brewed ale with the heavier taste of stronger old ale. See also: **India Pale Ale; porter.**

epergne A centrepiece for a formal dining table, usually constructed to display flowers or else hold dessert dishes or after-dinner sweetmeats.

epidemics The *Public Health Acts* of 1872 (35 & 36 Vict. c. 79) and 1875 (38 & 39 Vict. c. 55) were formulated in part as a response to the spread of epidemic disease, the former appointing medical officers for urban areas, and the latter establishing a coherent mechanism for the protection of health through proper sanitation: the 1875 Act required local authorities to oversee the provision of clean water, adequate drainage and the sanitary disposal of sewerage. See also: **cholera; typhoid fever; typhus**.

ether Deployed in **anaesthesia** by inhalation from 1846, ether was usually dripped onto a cloth covering the patient's nose and mouth or else inhaled through a nosepiece connected by a rubber tube to a sealed flask containing ether-soaked cotton wool.

Eton collar A stiff, detachable shirt collar, worn with its edges outside of the jacket, and named after the English **public school** where it was customarily worn as an item of uniform. The uniform for junior pupils at Eton, which featured a short jacket, was known as an Eton suit and was copied by many Victorian schools.

Eton fives Often abbreviated to 'fives', a handball game popular across the English **public school** system, the rules of which were formalised at Eton in 1877.

Eucharist The Christian sacrament of Holy Communion in which the sacrifice of Christ is recalled through a symbolic and communal consumption of bread and wine. The equivalent **Roman Catholic** sacrament of the Mass is regarded in some **Protestant** circles as theologically blasphemous, the thirty-first of the **Thirty-Nine Articles** of the **Anglican** Church openly proclaiming it as such.

euchre A popular card game for four players, playing in two teams with a numerically reduced deck of conventional playing cards. Initially omitted, the Joker was added to the euchre deck later in the nineteenth century. See also: **bridge; whist**.

evangelical A member of an essentially **Protestant** tendency in Christianity which prioritises a personal relationship with God and familiarity with the teachings of the Bible above participation in the ceremonies and rituals of the Church. Though missionary activities were undertaken by **high-church** Anglicans and **Roman Catholics**, evangelicals (both **dissenters** and **Anglicans**) were active in developing a presence in poorer urban areas in particular, the construction of churches and mission halls often being accompanied by educational, entertainment and youth activities which competed against the secular attractions of the **music hall** and the public house.

evensong An **Anglican** service, held in the afternoon or early evening, featuring hymns and readings and with no celebration of the **Eucharist**.

evolution Though popularised through the controversial reception of *On the Origin of Species by Means of Natural Selection* (1859) by Charles Darwin (1809–82), the concept of dynamic evolution had been discussed as a topic in European *Naturphilosophie* from the late eighteenth century. Darwin's writings, with those of Alfred Russell Wallace (1823–1913), however, made organic change a topic for wider discussion, and the well-reported (and rhetorically pointed) debate between Thomas Henry Huxley (1825–95) and Bishop Samuel Wilberforce (1805–73) at the 1860 meeting of the British Association for the Advancement of Science in Oxford did much to stimulate interest on the part of those who might never read a scientific book. The public debate served to distort the subtleties of Darwin's arguments, particularly through its persistent (and inaccurate) intimation that humanity is descended from the ape, rather than *both* of these species having a common and more distant ancestor.

F

fagging The historic practice in **public schools** (most notably in those institutions where boys are boarders rather than day pupils) in which younger scholars perform menial tasks – such as cleaning garments or shoes, cooking or shopping, or else maintaining a private study or sleeping quarters – at the behest of older pupils. Fagging, which dates from at least the seventeenth century, was supposed to inculcate humility and service as one of the ostensible virtues of *mens sana in corpore sano*, though the system was open to abuses that might range from physical and emotional bullying to actual sexual abuse. Fags, as the subaltern pupils were termed, appear to have been almost exclusively male – the practice of fagging was not widely adopted as female education expanded across the century.

farthing The smallest denomination coin in pre-decimal British **currency**, worth a quarter of a penny.

feather tray A flat tray, covered with black-dyed ostrich plumes, carried in advance of the hearse by a 'featherman' in Victorian **funeral**

processions. The plumes resembled those upon the hearse and the horses pulling the funeral vehicles and, if the deceased was an unmarried woman, might be white rather than black.

fellowship, college Within the collegiate system of the two ancient **universities** of Oxford and Cambridge, a fellow (who might be elected or appointed) was granted certain rights and privileges within his college. These might include accommodation, formal dining rights, and access to libraries or archives. Fellows were invariably male in the nineteenth century – women were not granted full access to university privileges until 1920 at Oxford and 1948 at Cambridge – and, until the 1828 *Sacramental Test Act* (9 Geo. 4 c. 17), were also required to be **Anglican** and, in many cases, both unmarried and ordained clergymen.

felo de se A **suicide**, the term emphasising that to kill oneself was a criminal act and thus punishable in law if unsuccessful. The 1882 *Interments (felo de se) Act* (45 & 46 Vict. c. 19) removed the earlier requirement that suicides be buried at night, in unconsecrated ground and without religious ceremony.

Fenian Colloquially, a member of the Irish Republican Brotherhood, a nationalist organisation founded in 1858 and committed to physical as well as political action against British rule in Ireland. A parallel American organisation, Clan na Gael, undertook raids into Canada in 1866 and 1870, was involved in the unsuccessful uprising in Ireland in 1867, and partially financed a bombing campaign in London in the 1880s. In Ireland, individual Fenians were involved in the **Irish National Land League** and in splinter groups such as the **Invincibles**.

fichu A triangular piece of fabric, often decorative and worn by women as a covering for the shoulders and chest.

field sports Outdoor sports, such as **hunting, beagling, pheasant shooting** and **deer stalking** which involve the pursuit and killing of **game** – wild animals or birds. Though the pursuit of quarry was central to field sports, the social aspect of hunting and shooting should be understood as having an almost equal importance due to the opportunities it presented, to those who could afford to participate regularly, for developing friendships, initiating romantic or dynastic relationships, and strengthening business interests. See also: **beater; gun**.

fin de siècle Derived from a French term meaning 'end of the century', this phrase is broadly applied to a period extending from the 1880s through to the first decade of the twentieth century. Through the writings of Max Nordau (1849–1923) in particular, fin-de-siècle manners, art and **Aestheticism** have been associated with **decadence** and cultural **degeneration,** and a pervasive Victorian perception that the period heralded 'the dusk of the nations'.

First War of [Indian] Independence See: **Indian Mutiny.**

fives See: **Eton fives.**

Fleet Prison Named after the subterranean River Fleet, a **debtors' prison** in London which also accommodated bankrupts and those charged with contempt of the courts of **Chancery,** Exchequer and Common Pleas. It was closed in 1842.

flogging An extreme form of whipping, often administered in public, regularly utilised as a punishment in the army, the navy, and the prison system for insubordination or dereliction of duty. Flogging, which could be fatal, was partially abolished in the Royal Navy in 1871, and fully discontinued in 1879; its punitive administration was abolished in the army in 1881. A less severe version of this corporal punishment, also known as birching or caning, was also routinely deployed in the public school system.

florin An English coin, to the value of two **shillings,** first minted in 1849. This Victorian coin should not be confused with the historical gold florin, first minted in 1344.

floriography See: **language of flowers.**

foot warmer A small metallic container into which hot water or glowing embers are placed in order to provide a source of heat for passengers travelling, for example, in an unheated coach or **railway** carriage.

footman A manservant, often dressed in **livery,** whose duty is to serve at the dining table or attend the coach of his employer.

Foresters, Ancient Order of See: **friendly society.**

Forster's Education Act The popular name for the 1870 *Elementary Education Act* (**33 & 34 Vict. c. 75**), which was drafted by the **Liberal** MP William Forster (1818–86). The Act expanded the provision of basic education in England and Wales, supplementing existing schools, including those provided by the **Anglican** Church, with new establishments managed by school boards, elected by local ratepayers. School attendance between the ages of five and thirteen was made compulsory in Scotland in 1872 under the *Education (Scotland) Act* (35 & 36 Vict. c. 62).

fox-hunting See: **hunting.**

Franklin Expedition A voyage of arctic exploration, led by Captain John Franklin, which left London in 1845 in search of an undiscovered **Northwest Passage** presumed to link the Atlantic and Pacific Oceans north of Canada. The aspirations of the expedition and the loss of the crew fed into a national myth of imperial heroism which served to counter rumours that suggested that the crew had variously starved or resorted to cannibalism.

free trade Trade or commerce conducted without restrictive duties, customs or taxes. The antithesis of protectionism, free trade was advantageous so long as the country maintained a market advantage in terms of production or cost. The repeal of the **Corn Laws** in 1846 marked the effective triumph of a business philosophy that had gained wide acceptance from around 1820, though some protectionist measures were retained until the **Liberal Party** budget of 1860 which reduced these to a nominal body of duties.

freeholder An individual who holds the absolute right of ownership of a piece of land, rather than merely occupying a building on it as a tenant or a leaseholder. Possession of a freehold worth 40 **shillings** per annum on the land tax valuation served as the defining property qualification for the franchise in rural counties prior to the **Reform Act** of 1832.

freemasonry A fraternal organisation for men, the symbolism of which is based upon the practice of medieval stonemasons. Freemasonry accompanied British soldiers, merchants and missionaries across the expanding British Empire, and its meetings facilitated social and professional contact between expatriates and non-Britons who were 'on the Square'. The essential qualification for membership was (and remains) a belief in a Supreme Being: as this term could be applied to any deity, Masonic lodges readily admitted Jews, Hindus and Muslims as well as Christians across the nineteenth century, as illustrated in the 1895 poem 'The Mother Lodge' by Rudyard Kipling (1865–1936).

friendly society A mutual insurance scheme into which individuals pay in anticipation of life assurance, sickness benefits or pensions. Like **burial clubs**, friendly societies attracted their primarily working-class and artisan subscribers with relatively low but regular payment schemes, and while some, such as the Ancient Order of Foresters (founded 1834), followed a fraternal model which resembled **Freemasonry**, others – such as the Liverpool Lyver Burial Society (founded 1850) – were based on primarily regional identities.

Figure 9 The funeral of Prince Albert. The hearse and horses display ostrich-feather plumes and the accompanying mutes carry short batons rather than staves. Engraving from the *Illustrated London News*, 28 December 1861.

full mourning The first and most profound state of **mourning** following a death. Conventionally, a middle-class widow would dress only in black and avoid social occasions for a minimum of a year and a day, with a subsequent period of **half mourning** to follow. Bourgeois widowers would likewise dress sombrely, albeit while undertaking any necessary engagement with the commercial world. Though the working classes were often extravagant in the pursuit of a **funeral** appropriate to the memory of the deceased, economic necessity reduced the conventional imperatives which confined grieving relatives to the home following a death.

funerals See also: **feather tray; full mourning; half mourning; mourning; mute; undertaker.**

furlong A distance of 220 yards (201.168 metres). There are eight furlongs to a mile.

fustian A coarse and hardwearing fabric, usually of made of cotton, and suitable for industrial or agricultural work clothing.

G

game Though the term may be generically applied to hunted deer, the 1831 *Game Act* (1 & 2 Will. 4 c. 32) limits its legal application to hares and wild birds. The 1831 Act prohibited the shooting of partridge between 1 February and 1 September; pheasant between 1 February to 1 October; grouse between 10 December and 12 August; and bustard between 1 March to 1 September, annually. The Act also maintained the legal requirement of formal certification for those taking (that is, **shooting** or trapping) game, and those dealing in game as a foodstuff. This requirement effectively criminalised poachers – those who took game without permission – and limited access to game-shooting to individuals who could afford a licence. The shooting of rabbit and pigeon – which are both classified as vermin rather than game – was not regulated under the Act. See also: **field sports**.

gamp Colloquially, an umbrella. The name derives from the inebriate Sarah Gamp in *Martin Chuzzlewit* (1843–4) by Charles Dickens (1812–70).

gaslight See: **coal gas**.

gay A derogatory term applied to a woman whose livelihood is based upon **prostitution**, or whose sexual reputation has been questioned in some other way. Beyond these associations, a 'gay' horse is one that is excessively spirited and difficult to control, where a hound may be described as having a 'gay' tail when that member is carried erect. See also: **hunting**.

gentleman ranker A member of a military regiment or colonial police force who, though educated as a gentleman, is serving in the ranks rather than as an officer.

gentlemen and players In **cricket**, the distinction between financially independent individuals who play the game as amateurs (gentlemen) and those who receive payment for their participation (players).

gig A light two-wheeled carriage, drawn by one horse. See also: **dog cart**.

gin palace A derogatory term applied to a gaudily decorated public house, though not necessarily one associated only with the sale of gin. Gin palaces characteristically catered to a primarily working-class clientele, were often brightly illuminated with **coal gas**, and were decorated with mirrors, frosted glass and polychromatic tilework inside and out.

Girl of the Period An anti-feminist parody created by the journalist Elizabeth Lynn Linton (1822–98), and named as such in an essay first published in the *Saturday Review* in 1868. The Girl of the Period anticipated the **New Woman** with her independence and sexual forwardness, eschewing modest living for luxury, marrying for personal advantage rather than love, and rejecting the supposedly innate gendered imperatives which ostensibly tied her sex to motherhood and the **domestic sphere**. Her taste for radical fashion was further demonised through racist terminology and the suggestion that deviance from the gendered norm represented a form of madness and **degeneration**.

Girl's Own Paper, The A parallel publication to *The Boys' Own Paper*, the G.O.P. (as it was customarily abbreviated) appeared weekly from 1880 and entertained its readers with a diet of wholesome stories and educational articles. Published by the **Religious Tract Society**, and edited by a man – Charles Peters (d. 1907) – the magazine featured a regular column, entitled 'Answers to Correspondents', where the female reader might seek advice anonymously on topics ranging from medical issues to the difficulties of domestic or school life.

Girton College The first residential **university**-level residential college for women in Britain, founded in 1869 within the University of Cambridge, and the immediate predecessor of **Newnham College**, Cambridge, which opened in 1871. Girton was the model for **Somerville College** and **Lady Margaret Hall**, Oxford, both of which were established in 1879. See also: **clubs**.

Girton girl An often derogatory term describing a 'Girtonite' or student of **Girton College**, Cambridge. Women studying at Girton in particular were parodied, in writing and through cartoon imagery in *Punch* and elsewhere, as superficially attractive but intellectually shallow 'sweet girl graduates' or else serious and unfeminine rhetoricians incongruously emulating nominally masculine manners and pastimes.

Gladstone bag A travelling bag with a rigid frame, hinged and opening at the top, popular from mid-century. Often made of leather, the bag was named after the statesman William Ewart Gladstone (1809–98).

glanders A contagious disease of horses, which causes swelling of the jaw and a nasal discharge.

Figure 10 Cover of *The Girl's Own Paper*, 4 October 1884.

Glasgow School A stylistically influential group of artists, working in Scotland from the 1880s, whose work is often associated with both the **Arts and Crafts movement** and **art nouveau**. Though sometimes derided as the 'Spook School', on account of its taste for Celtic motifs and stylised human figures, the work of Charles Rennie Mackintosh (1868–1928) and his close associates should be contemplated as being culturally discrete from English and European practice particularly in the design of decorative metalwork, and in the application of its customary motifs to commercial interiors (Miss Cranston's Tea Rooms, Glasgow, 1896) and domestic architecture (The Hill House, Helensburgh, 1902).

Glorious Twelfth The twelfth of August, which marks the opening of the shooting season for red grouse under the 1831 *Game Act* (1 & 2 Will. 4 c. 4). See also: **field sports**.

Golden Dawn The popular name for the Hermetic Order of the Golden Dawn, an occult society for men and women founded in 1887. The order's ceremonial procedure was partially derived from **Freemasonry** – its original founders all being Freemasons – and it proved particularly attractive to authors and poets, both Arthur Machen (1863–1947) and William Butler Yeats (1865–1939) being initiated as members, as well as to an educated coterie interested in mysticism and **theosophy**.

gombeenism An form of unregulated usury, practised by both sexes – individual practitioners being described as a gombeenman or gombeenwoman – largely confined to poorer and primarily agricultural areas of Ireland.

Gothic novel A genre of primarily supernatural fiction, first named as such in 1765 and popularised through an enduring presence within the **circulating library** system. Though the so-called First Phase of Gothic is critically assumed to have ended with the publication of *Frankenstein* in 1818, the Gothic's conventions of sublime landscapes and characterisation were perpetuated through **Romanticism**, and informed not merely popular genres such as **melodrama**, the **penny dreadful** and crime fiction but also newspaper reportage and social reporting. Gothic fiction returned to popularity in the second half of the century in part as a consequence of the frequent appearance of ghost stories in weekly and monthly journals.

Gothic Revival architecture Regarded as a northern and **Protestant** alternative to the Classical architecture of Greece and Rome by both civic and church authorities, the details of medieval Gothic were applied by Victorian designers not merely to stone but also to brick, cast iron and decorative ceramics. Popularised in part by the **Commissioners' Gothic** of the earlier century, the style was adopted for the reconstructed Houses of Parliament (completed 1870), nominally designed by Charles Barry (1795–1860) but with significant assistance from the **Roman Catholic** designer Augustus Welby Pugin, in order to symbolically balance governmental tradition with the contemporary administration. Similar imperatives may be associated with the deployment of Gothic in British **railway** terminals: travellers to or from St Pancras Station (opened 1868) were accommodated in a Gothic Revival hotel (opened 1876) whose fixtures signified the comforts of an idealised past, though the journey itself began or ended in a glazed train-shed the modernity of which recalled the contemporary **Crystal Palace**.

gout A form of inflammatory arthritis which causes acute pain in the joints, particularly that of the great toe. Popularly associated with excessive eating and drinking – red meat and **port** being especially suspect – gout was treated primarily through the imposition of a restricted diet, and its pain eased by the use of specially adapted furniture, such as the 'gout stool', which removed pressure from the affected part.

governess An unmarried woman responsible for the formal and moral education of a child or children in a private household. Governesses typically occupied a peculiar social position in the domestic environment. Though they were both paid and accommodated for their service, they were usually much better educated than their fellow **servants**. They often dined not in the servants' hall but with the children in their care, and though they might also join their employers at table, they could never be considered unequivocal members of the family.

grammar schools Slightly less prestigious than the great **public schools**, grammar schools were private institutions which educated their male pupils in a liberal – rather than scientific or technical – curriculum which typically included instruction in Latin and often in Greek also. The term is customarily used to describe schools of great antiquity – such as King Edward VI School in Stratford-upon-Avon, established in the thirteenth century, as well as Victorian foundations such as the Liverpool Collegiate

Figure 11 Harvey Lonsdale Elmes's Tudor-Gothic design for the façade of the Liverpool Collegiate, a Victorian grammar school founded in 1840 and opened in 1843. Engraving in the *Illustrated London News*, 14 January 1843.

School (founded 1840). Though admission to a grammar school was based nominally upon the ability to pay the requisite fees, many institutions admitted pupils upon subsidised bursaries or without fees as an act of public charity. A late-Victorian tradition of new grammar schools for girls – such as Simon Langton Girls' School, Canterbury (founded 1881) – often drew upon the paradigm of earlier, and exclusively male, establishments. It should be noted that, in twentieth-century British usage, the term 'grammar school' was applied to selective institutions, usually managed by a local authority or religious denomination, which did not charge fees.

Grand National, the The successor to the Grand Liverpool **Steeplechase**, which was first run in 1829, the Grand National has been run at Aintree since at least 1839, and possibly at a former racecourse at Maghull for two years prior to that date.

Grand Old Man Sometimes abbreviated G.O.M., a nickname for the statesman William Ewart Gladstone (1809–98). Following the death of Major-General Charles George Gordon (1833–85), some critics of the statesman's supposed inactivity during the Siege of Khartoum reputedly inverted the abbreviation in order to declare Gladstone the 'murderer of Gordon'.

Great Exhibition, the 'The Great Exhibition of the Works of Industry of All Nations' took place in London's Hyde Park between 1 May and 11 October 1851, attracting around six million visitors to the prefabricated **Crystal Palace** in which its approximately 100,000 exhibits were housed. Though nominally international, the event emphasised both British industrial innovation and its expression through artistic media, and fulfilled an educative function for the working and artisan classes when the admission price was reduced to one **shilling** on 24 May. The influence popularly assumed to have been exerted by Prince Albert over the whole project is probably no underestimate: royal patronage made the event not merely fashionable but lucrative, the profit of £186,000 underwriting the construction of the new museums of **Albertopolis**.

Great Stink A two-month period spanning July and August 1858 in which unusually hot weather caused the domestic refuse, industrial effluent and human excrement associated with the River Thames and its banks to odorously decompose. A prevailing fear of infection, which recalled the memory of comparatively recent outbreaks of **cholera** in the capital, led to practical intervention into the London sewerage system and the construction of waterside embankments under designs originated by Joseph Bazalgette (1819–91) which inhibited the accumulation of waste on the river's banks.

Greater Britain The British Empire beyond Great Britain and Ireland, particularly when being discussed in contexts relevant to cultural integration or **imperial federation**.

greenery-yallary Extracted from a line in the **Savoy Opera** *Patience* (1881) – 'a greenery-yallery, **Grosvenor Gallery**, foot-in-the-grave young man' – a term of contempt for the **fin-de-siècle** culture and taste of **Aestheticism** generally, based upon two of the movement's predominant colours. See also: **yellow**.

groat The popular, but *not* official, name for a coin minted between 1836 and 1856 with a value of four pennies. See also: **currency**.

groom A servant who attends to horses and their associated tack. The term was also widely deployed as an abbreviation of bridegroom.

Figure 12 The genesis of the Great Stink: the River Thames as common sewer. 'The water that John drinks'. Cartoon from *Punch*, 13 October 1849.

Grosvenor Gallery An art gallery in New Bond Street, London, which exhibited works by the **Pre-Raphaelites** and became a focus for **Aestheticism** between 1877 and 1890.

grouse shooting See: game.

growler A four-wheeled horse-drawn cab, reputedly so called because of the noise made by its wheels on **cobblestones** or setts.

gruel A cheap and semi-liquid food, primarily composed of oatmeal mixed with water or milk, and associated in particular with the punitive regimes of prisons and **workhouses**.

guinea A unit of currency comprising one pound and one **shilling** (21/-). Coins with a nominal value of one guinea were minted only between 1663 and 1813 in association with African colonisation and **slavery**, though the convention of charging professional fees in guineas was retained by **physicians, surgeons** and lawyers, and persisted also in the prizes offered in some competitive sports and in horse racing.

gun In field sports this term may refer to the firearm itself – typically a smooth-bore shotgun in grouse or **pheasant shooting** or a rifle in **deer stalking** – or the individual who is using it. In driven grouse and pheasant shoots, a gun would frequently employ a loader, who would reload a second shot gun while its counterpart was being fired.

gutta percha A type of natural latex widely used in the manufacture of artificial jet for **mourning jewellery** and in the gum structure of dentures. See also: **Waterloo teeth**.

H

habeas corpus Though this term is associated with a specific legal act of 1679, its popular place in British culture is as an emblem for the assumption that an individual cannot be held indefinitely without trial, and that any trial will serve also to determine the legality of the imprisonment. Culturally, the juridical suspension of habeas corpus has long been regarded as an affront to the traditional liberty enjoyed by the citizen, and an implicit declaration of the absolute power or tyranny of the state.

hackney carriage A horse-drawn carriage, usually on four wheels and drawn by two horses, available for public hire. See also: **growler; hansom cab**.

half mourning The second stage of **mourning**, which follows the period known as **full mourning**. At this stage, between eighteen months and two years following bereavement, the widow's hitherto wholly black garments may be supplemented with muted shades such as grey, lavender or white for a period of around six months. A widower might relieve the darkness of his business suit with a lighter necktie or a grey, rather than black, top hat. Social distinction inevitably impacted upon the length and nature of mourning for both sexes, and if the working-class preference was often for elaborate and costly **funerals**, extended periods of abstinence from work were limited by economic necessity.

Hampden clubs A loose organisation of working-class radical societies, first organised in 1812, and agitating through meetings and petitions for political reform. Though essentially autonomous, the clubs attracted the suspicion of both local and national government and were suppressed in 1817.

Hansard A printed account of debates, divisions and votes in the **House of Commons** and **House of Lords**. The name is derived from Thomas Curson Hansard (1776–1833), who published the debates from 1812, and entered into popular usage in 1889. Parliamentary speeches are reproduced almost verbatim in *Hansard*, with verbal interjections from the Chamber, such as cheers, being duly recorded in passing.

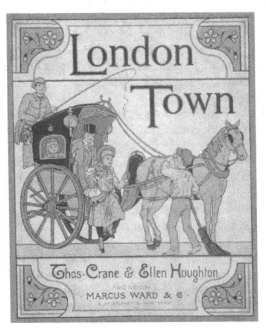

Figure 13 Hansom cab and street Arab crossing sweeper, depicted on the cover of Thomas Crane and Ellen Houghton, *London Town* (1883).

hansom cab A two-wheeled, one-horse carriage, the driver of which is seated above the passenger compartment on a so-called 'dickey seat'. See also: **growler; hackney carriage.**

hard labour Heavy (and often pointless) physical work – such as **stone-breaking,** working on the **treadmill** or turning a crank – punitively imposed upon a prison sentence. Similar activities were on occasions employed with the **workhouse** system. See also: **oakum.**

hare coursing A **field sport** in which a hare is pursued across a 'running ground' by two greyhounds under the gaze of a mounted judge. The rules of the National Coursing Club, founded in 1858, state that the aim is not for the greyhounds (which hunt by sight) to actually *catch* the hare, but rather for them to *pursue* it accurately as it rapidly changes direction during the chase and attempts to escape by way of artificial refuges known as 'soughs' or natural conduits called 'meuses'. See also: **Waterloo Cup.**

hatchment A diamond- or lozenge-shaped plaque upon which is painted a representation of the coat of arms of a deceased member of the gentry or nobility. Usually provided by the **undertaker,** the hatchment was traditionally displayed over the front door of the residence until the **funeral** had taken place. It was then displayed in the **parish** church until the funerary monument had been installed, though many continued to be displayed following this latter event.

hatter See: **millinery.**

havelock A cloth addition to a cap or kepi, which hangs down to protect the back of the wearer's neck from exposure to the sun.

high church An identity within the **Anglican** Church which favours elaborate ritual and clerical dress, often reminiscent of **Roman Catholic** practice, rather than the more simple **Protestant** tradition of the evangelicals. See also: **broad church; Oxford Movement.**

Hobson-Jobson A glossary of Anglo-Indian words and colloquialisms, published by Henry Yule and Arthur Coke Burnell in 1886.

hock A white wine from Germany, often medium rather than truly dry in taste, popular in England across the nineteenth century.

hodge A term commonly applied when generalising about the demeanour, behaviour or fate of the English agricultural labourer. 'Drummer Hodge' (1899) by Thomas Hardy (1840–1928) depicts one such figure as a victim of the Second **Boer War.**

hokey-pokey A colloquial name for ice cream, particularly that sold by street vendors.

PUNCH, OR THE LONDON CHARIVARI.—October 24, 1868.

THE CHICHESTER EXTINGUISHER.

Bishop of Chichester. "GO! GO! YOU INSOLENT, REBELLIOUS BOY. WHAT WITH YOUR NONSENSE AND INCENSE AND CANDLES YOU'LL BE SETTING THE CHURCH ON FIRE."

Master P-ch-s. "JUST WHAT I'D LIKE TO DO. THERE!"

Figure 14 The Anglican Bishop of Chichester (right) admonishes a high-church cleric for ritualist practices. Cartoon from *Punch*, 24 October 1868.

Holywell Street A London thoroughfare which ran parallel to The Strand and was associated with both radical political booksellers and the lucrative trade in **pornography**. The area was redeveloped at the turn of the twentieth century and the street removed.

Home Rule A long-running political movement, campaigning for the self-governance of Ireland and the restoration of a parliament in Dublin. A Home Government Association was founded in Ireland in 1870, and a Home Rule League in 1873, which successfully contested parliamentary elections across Ireland. In England, the cause of Home Rule was taken up by William Ewart Gladstone (1809–98) in 1885 and by others within the **Liberal Party**, but opposed by many **Liberal Unionists** and **Conservatives**. Viewed with suspicion by many **Protestants** in England and Scotland, who feared the imposition of a **Roman Catholic** hierarchy, Home Rule was vigorously opposed outside of Parliament by **Orangemen** in all three countries, who organised demonstrations and mobilised voters. Unsuccessful bills proposing Home Rule were submitted to Parliament by Gladstone in 1886 and 1893, and the issue effectively split the Liberal Party in the

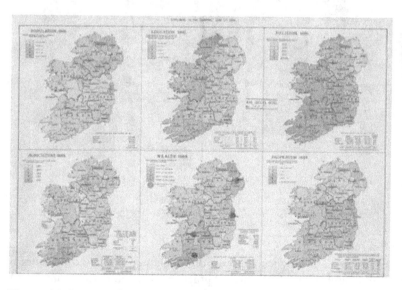

Figure 15 Statistical map of Ireland covering 1881–5. Supplement to *The Graphic*, 5 June 1886.

later century and increased its legislative dependence upon Irish Members of Parliament.

homosexuality Same-sex desire in the nineteenth century was policed by way of the legal system (which viewed it as a punishable offence); through medicine (which understood it as a deviance from the reproductive and heterosexual norm); and by the Church (which configured it as a sin to be preached against). Under such scrutiny, it was inevitable that underground networks would develop, particularly within the many gender-exclusive organisations – such as the army, navy and **universities** – which structured professional and social contact in the period. In law, a conviction for sodomy *could* in theory be followed by a sentence of **capital punishment** until the passing of the 1861 *Offences Against the Person Act* (**24 & 25 Vict. c. 100**), though it would appear that most of those prosecuted were imprisoned, often with **hard labour**, rather than summarily executed. The provisions of the 1885 **Labouchère Amendment** made the prosecution (and effective persecution) of homosexual men considerably easier by removing the need for proof that sodomy had itself actually occurred: essentially, even gatherings of homosexual men might be construed as constituting a form of 'gross indecency'. Medically, homosexuality was frequently claimed as a likely consequence of uncorrected **onanism,** this latter act also being viewed as deviant by many within the Church. It must be stressed that the bulk of legislation was directed explicitly towards male same-sex desire, which was later termed **uranism**: lesbianism (sometimes termed 'Sapphism'), though contemplated in medical writings, did not substantially inform the legal debate and was largely ignored also by the Church.

hookah pipe A pipe for smoking flavoured tobacco. The tobacco is burned on charcoal, and the smoke is cooled by being passed through water before it is inhaled through a mouthpiece connected to a flexible rubber tube.

horseless carriage A road vehicle powered either by steam or else an internal combustion engine. Steam traction engines and road locomotives became popular from the 1860s. Effective internal combustion engines were developed from the 1870s, and the first petrol-powered three- and four-wheeled motor vehicles appeared on British roads from 1894, and were initially limited to a maximum speed of four miles per hour (6.4 km/h) under the 1865 *Locomotives Act* (28 & 29 Vict. c. 83).

house of assignation A brothel, or on occasion a place where illicit or extramarital love affairs are carried out.

House of Commons The elected legislative chamber governing Britain, Scotland and Ireland following the *Acts of Union* of 1707 and 1800. The composition, both socially and numerically, of the Chamber was affected by the three Reform Acts of 1832 (2 & 3 Will. 4 c. 45), 1867 (<u>30 & 31 Vict. c. 102</u>) and 1884 (<u>48 & 49 Vict. c. 3</u>), as well as the 1885 *Redistribution of Seats Act* (<u>48 & 49 Vict. c. 23</u>) which attempted to equalise the size of electoral constituencies. See also: **House of Lords.**

house of correction A prison or **bridewell**, the name implying that those imprisoned will in theory be reformed as well as punished.

House of Lords The hereditary legislative chamber of the United Kingdom, which reviews, amends and either passes or else rejects legislation that has been approved by the **House of Commons.** The composition of the Chamber was based in part upon lineage, some nineteenth-century English Lords Temporal having gained that right on account of **peerages** awarded centuries before. The peers of Ireland and Scotland did *not* enjoy an automatic right to sit in the Lords, and instead elected representatives from among their numbers. An English or Scottish peer could not sit as a Member of Parliament in the House of Commons, though an Irish peer was allowed to do so if elected. In addition to the Lords Temporal, votes could be cast within the House by the Lords Spiritual – some (but not all) of the bishops of the **Anglican** Church – and by the Lords of Appeal in Ordinary, colloquially known as the Law Lords, who oversaw the juridical prerogative which the Chamber exercised in addition to its legislative function: the House of Lords was the highest Court of Appeal in the country.

Houses of Parliament An umbrella term by which the legislature of the **House of Commons** and the **House of Lords** is collectively described. Colloquially, the term is often applied to the buildings which make up the Palace of Westminster in which Parliament is physically housed.

housekeeper The most senior female **servant,** and the counterpart of the male **butler** in larger households. Housekeepers consulted on an essentially daily basis with the mistress of the house with regard to the management of the **domestic sphere,** oversaw the provisioning of the larder in consultation with the cook, and maintained good conduct among the female servants; the discipline of male servants fell to the butler. In houses without male servants, the housekeeper's role and influence were likely to be somewhat more extensive. See also: **maid of all work.**

hoyden A seventeenth-century term for a rude or badly behaved girl, which still enjoyed a level of currency and application in nineteenth-century literary culture.

Hudson's Bay Company A commercial organisation incorporated in England in 1670 to engage in exploration – specifically to find the **Northwest Passage** – and to exploit the natural resources of Canada, including the lucrative fur trade. Like the **East India Company,** the Company eventually saw its trading monopoly removed (in 1859), and it sold the substantial territory which it controlled to the Canadian Government in 1870, receiving in exchange a financial settlement accompanied by a number of territorial grants, which included mineral and trading rights, that permitted its continuance as a viable commercial entity.

hulk See: **prison hulk.**

humbug An emphatic interjection, the use of which is associated with the belief that some statement or action is not genuine but a sham or an imposture.

hunter In British **hunting,** this term is usually applied to a *horse* suited to hunting rather than an individual engaged in **field sports** or the pursuit of **game.** A hunter pocket watch (sometimes called a hunter case watch) is a timepiece, often suspended from an **albert,** which features a spring-restrained cover that protects the dial from scratches or damage; a half-hunter watch includes a glass panel in the cover through which the dial might be viewed while the cover is closed.

hunting In British use, this term is usually applied without prefix *only* to fox hunting on horseback: stag and otter hunting are always qualified through the name of the quarry species, whereas **field sports** which involve an individual pursuing **game** with a shotgun are designated **shooting.** Hunting is not merely an outdoor activity but also involves those who subscribe to a hunt in an elaborate calendar of social activities. The expensive nature of hunting – in addition to the annual cost of the subscription, a financial 'cap' is customarily paid for each day spent in the field, to which must be added the purchase of clothing, plus the maintenance of the horses, their stabling and tack – necessarily limited actual participation to the wealthy. The culture of hunting, though, became widely known through the comedic fictions of, among others, R. S. Surtees (1805–64), Edith Somerville (1858–1949) and the (pseudonymous) Martin Ross (1862–1915), as well as the parodying of hunting songs in the urban **music hall**. Hunting was practised across the British Empire: the Ootacamund **Club** (founded 1841) established a hunt in 1848 which remains active.

hunting box A small house or cottage occupied during the **hunting** season.

hunting pink The skirted red coat traditionally worn by Masters of Foxhounds, huntsmen and **whippers-in** while engaged in mounted **hunting**. The term is not universal, with red or scarlet also used to describe the garment in some Victorian accounts.

Hyde Park Riots Following the recent failure of a franchise reform bill, the Reform League proposed holding a rally in Hyde Park, London, on 23 July 1866. The meeting was banned by the **Conservative** Home Secretary, and though the League marched to the gates on the day, they avoided a confrontation with the police and diverted to Trafalgar Square. A group of protestors remained behind, however and, as the gates were locked, pulled down the perimeter railings in several places to gain entry to the park. Violence continued for several days in the vicinity of the park, damage was done to its facilities, and to houses in adjacent Belgravia, and the episode informed the influential study *Culture and Anarchy* (1869) by Matthew Arnold (1822–88).

hypnotism Strictly speaking, this term should not be applied to **mesmerism**, but only to the physiologically based practice popularised by the **surgeon** James Braid (1795–1860) from the 1840s. James Esdaile (1808-1859), an **East India Company** surgeon, employed hypnotism as a surgical anaesthetic on the Subcontinent in the same decade.

hysteria Regarded for much of the century as a gender-specific disease confined to women, hysteria was a matter of concern for both established physiological medicine and the nascent discipline of psychology. Associated in particular with a perceived biological destiny for the female body in heterosexual congress and reproduction, hysteria was an easy diagnosis to impose upon unmarried but sexually curious young women as well as older spinsters: marriage (the only sanctioned form of sexual fulfilment for women) was often encouraged as a putative cure. The conventional symptoms of hysteria included a persistent sensation of choking (the descendent of a much earlier definition of hysteria

Figure 16 A mid-century mounted hunt meets at a country house. John Everett Millais, 'Monkton Grange' from Anthony Trollope, *Orley Farm* (1861–2).

in which a rising *globus hystericus* was assumed to restrict the airways), and intimations of abdominal pains and blockages; a tendency to languor, possibly accompanied by fainting fits (syncope); and on occasion a taste for unusual or inedible substances (pica). The **physician** Robert Brudenell Carter (1828–1918) theorised the disorder in *On the Pathology and Treatment of Hysteria* (1853), configuring it as a mental illness that precedes in three stages, the last of which – tertiary hysteria – is structured as nothing less than the practice of attention-seeking imposture on the part of the female patient. Though supposedly 'effeminate' young men and **onanists** were on occasion diagnosed as hysterics, Jean-Martin Charcot (1825–93) was to later extend the diagnosis of traumatic hysteria to male patients, such as **railway** workers, who enjoyed robust physicality.

I

ice house An insulated building, usually constructed partially underground, in which ice was stored prior to the introduction of domestic refrigeration in larger country houses.

illegitimacy Often signified by the absence of any paternal name in the **parish** baptismal register or, following the introduction of a civil register of births in 1837, on the formal certificate of birth, bastardy had legal implications for inheritance, particularly as parentage might not be proved through anything other than circumstantial evidence. The 1834 *Poor Law Amendment Act* (4 & 5 Will. 4 c. 76) permitted the pursuit of the fathers of illegitimate children for the costs of maintenance if the child was deemed dependent upon the parish for relief.

Imperial Federation League Formed in 1884, an organisation which aspired to transform the existing British Empire into a federation of states governed by separate parliaments. As a response to the emergence of local nationalisms, the League implicitly endorsed the continued ascendancy of white colonial culture across the Empire, and its principles gained support most notably in Canada, Australia, New Zealand and the West Indies. Though the League existed as a campaigning organisation in Britain only until 1894, its influence upon politics was enduring, being illustrated most significantly in the successive conferences of colonial premiers which began in 1887.

imperial preference A response to the declining fortunes of free trade in the 1890s – a decade in which the competitiveness of British industry was specifically threatened by Germany and the United States – imperial preference was a political doctrine which proposed the imposition of reciprocally lower tariffs for goods traded between the nations of the Empire, thereby granting the United Kingdom and its colonies a trading advantage over non-imperial competitors.

in loco parentis From the Latin, meaning 'in the place of a parent', this legal term denotes the responsibility which an adult who is not a blood relative may exercise over an individual under the age of **majority**. Such responsibilities frequently encompassed not merely a commitment to formally educate or train but also an imperative to provide moral instruction. Thus, a **university** tutor would act *in loco parentis* for any undergraduate under the age of twenty-one years, an employer would stand in the same relationship to an apprentice, as would a military or naval officer in respect of young recruits under their command.

income tax Abolished following the end of the Napoleonic Wars in 1816, income tax was reintroduced at a rate of 7 pence in the pound by the 1842 Budget, albeit only on those whose annual incomes exceeded £150. Though both Benjamin Disraeli (1804–81) and William Ewart Gladstone (1809–98) proposed the abolition of the tax, it remained in force, with varying rates and not as a form of mass taxation.

indentured labour A form of contract labour which developed in part as a consequence of the abolition of **slavery**. Indentured labourers – often derogatively generalised as '**coolies**' – were sourced from India, China and elsewhere in Asia, and contracted to work for a set period of years either on plantations or else in the construction of colonial infrastructure such as **railways**. Such a contract usually allocated wages, accommodation and possibly a return ticket home, though these agreements were not always fulfilled by employers.

India Pale Ale [or, sometimes, East India Pale Ale] A bitter-tasting beer, often abbreviated to IPA, brewed with hops and usually having a relatively high alcohol content. Both the hops and the strength of the beer helped preserve it during the sea voyages on which it was shipped to supply British civilians and military garrisons in colonial India.

Indian club A heavy, bottle-shaped implement which is swung – usually in pairs – during physical exercises to strengthen the arms. It is likely that Indian clubs were introduced to Britain by soldiers returning from the Subcontinent during the first two decades of the century.

Indian Mutiny Also known as the Sepoy Mutiny and – increasingly – the First War of Independence, this was a rising by the indigenous population of India against the rule of the **East India Company** initially in Meerut, and latterly across the Subcontinent between May 1857 and June 1858. Support for the rising was uneven, and the reasons which prompted it complex and not uniform across India. The defeat of the rising prompted the British Government to end **John Company** Rule in India, and to implicate the Subcontinent in a **raj** system that was profitably imperial rather than being merely advantageous to those subscribing to the proprietary **joint-stock company**.

Indian tonic water Invented around 1825, a mixture of soda water, sugar and quinine which was originally added to gin as a prophylactic against malaria by soldiers stationed in India.

indoor relief Support, including food, accommodation and clothing, supplied under the **Poor Law** to the inmates of a **workhouse** as opposed to **outdoor relief**, the receipt of which permitted the indigent poor to remain in their current homes.

Inns of Court Located in London, the four Inns of Court – Gray's Inn, the Inner Temple, Lincoln's Inn and the Middle Temple – are the only bodies permitted to appoint (or 'call') **barristers** for service in the legal courts of England and Wales. In the manner of the colleges of the ancient **universities**, they fulfil a residential as well as a tutorial function. See also: **bencher**.

insolvency See: **bankruptcy**.

inst. An abbreviation often used in business correspondence, which refers to a date in the current month. For example, a request for payment on 'the 20th inst.' would indicate to the recipient that payment is due on the twentieth day of the month in which the bill had been issued.

intramural burial The interment of cadavers within the structural boundary of a church or other place of worship. Many churches were constructed over crypts or vaults in which bodies might be interred at a cost higher than that associated with extramural burial in the churchyard, and in some cases these were owned by, or reserved in the names of, wealthy or notable families associated with the **parish**. The traditional fear of the infectious miasmas supposed to emanate from dead bodies, even from those encased in **lead coffins**, was enhanced by the presence of insects visibly emerging from crypts such as that underlying London's Enon **Chapel** in the 1840s. The 1850 *Metropolitan Interments Act* (13 & 14 Vict. c. 52) and subsequent legislation severely restricted intramural burial within the capital, closed many overcrowded city churchyards, and facilitated the development of large cemeteries beyond its most densely populated areas, with corresponding action regarding the hygienic disposal of the dead being undertaken outside of London from mid-century. See also: **cremation; funerals.**

Inverness cape A removable cape, worn over an overcoat.

Invincibles An Irish nationalist organisation active between 1881 and 1883. Two members of the group committed the Phoenix Park Murders on 6 May 1882, fatally stabbing the British Chief Secretary for Ireland and the Permanent Under Secretary with surgical knives.

Irish National Land League Founded by Michael Davitt (1846–1906) in 1879 as an initially agrarian reform movement in Ireland, the Land League became associated with broader nationalist politics in part through the leadership of Charles Stewart Parnell (1846–91). See also: **Irish National League.**

Irish National League Formed by Charles Stewart Parnell (1846–91) in 1882 as a successor to the **Irish National Land League**, which had been declared illegal that year, the League supported the work of Irish **Home Rule** politicians in Parliament, with the specific endorsement of the **Roman Catholic** hierarchy in Ireland. The League was fractured, and the commitment of the Church disturbed, by allegations of adultery directed against Parnell in 1890.

irregular marriage Under Scottish law (which is a system discrete from its English and Irish counterparts), a marriage contracted not through a religious or civil ceremony but by the simple expedient of declaring the same in front of two witnesses.

J

Jack Tar A popular generic personification of the British sailor, particularly a serving member of the Royal Navy.

Jack the Ripper The supposed perpetrator of the **Whitechapel Murders** of 1888, the name originated in a letter so-signed and sent to the Central News Agency that year.

Jamaica Rebellion An eleven-day revolt by **slaves** on the British colonial island of Jamaica which began on 25 December 1831. Organised largely through a network of **dissenting** Christian missions, most notably those professing a local interpretation of Baptist theology, and motivated in part by the frustration of their requests for emancipation, the rebels captured large areas of rural Jamaica, and attacked and burned several **sugar** estates before martial law was declared by the colonial authorities. British rule was restored with the assistance of emancipated slaves – the Maroons – and reprisals against the enslaved population included summary execution and the burning of missionary **chapels**.

Jameson Raid An incursion into the **Boer** republic of Transvaal by British settlers from Cape Colony under Leander Starr Jameson (1853–1917) spanning 1895–6. A telegram sent by Kaiser Wilhelm II of Germany to Paul Kruger (1825–1904) on 3 January 1896, congratulating the president of the Transvaal on the defeat of the intended coup, was interpreted by many in Britain as confirmation of German imperial ambitions.

japanned A surface that has been varnished or lacquered in order to make it resemble the typically black and shiny appearance associated with historical Japanese furniture.

Jermyn Street A fashionable commercial thoroughfare in **St James's** area of London, popularly associated with the bespoke tailoring and sale of gentlemen's clothing as well as **hatters** and perfumers. Jermyn Street also housed at least two exclusive and male-only **Turkish baths**.

jet A type of fossilised coal, associated in particular with Whitby in Yorkshire, which was polished and used in the manufacture of **mourning jewellery**. See also: **gutta percha**.

jingoism An expression used to denote populist patriotism, particularly in the mass media. The phrase comes from the **music hall** song 'We Don't Want to Fight' by George William Hunt (c. 1838–1904) and came into popular use around 1877–8.

John Bull A personification of the English nation (and, in some interpretations, the four nations of the United Kingdom) in the form of a genial but physically resilient country gentleman. Typically, in his Victorian incarnation, John Bull wears a tailcoat, top hat and brown-tipped **top boots** such as might be worn when **hunting**, and in some cases a waistcoat fashioned from the Union Flag. Possibly less well known are his three

Figure 17 John Bull in the company of the three male personifications of the United Kingdom: Pat, Sandy and Taffy. Undated anti-Home Rule post-card.

national associates: Pat, the Irishman; Sandy, the kilted Scot; and Taffy, the Welshman.

John Company A humorous name which effectively personified the **East India Company**.

joint-stock company A mode of commercial organisation in which the stock or capital is contributed and owned by a number of individuals jointly as a common fund. The extensive membership of joint-stock companies meant that any legal action in which it was involved had to be undertaken in the joint names of all the members, and further that each member might be liable to potentially unlimited losses should the company fail. These difficulties were addressed in legislation in 1844 (7 & 8 Vict. c. 110) and 1856 (19 & 20 Vict. c. 47).

jubilee Popularly, a public celebration and, in nineteenth-century usage, most commonly associated with the longevity of Queen Victoria's reign between 1837 and 1901. The Golden Jubilee was formally celebrated by the Queen on 20 and 21 June 1887 and the Diamond Jubilee on 22 June 1897, although public celebrations in London and the provinces extended throughout the years in question and were marked by banquets, the dedication of buildings and the opening of civic facilities such as art galleries and museums.

Juggernaut A title of the Indian deity Krishna, which may also be spelled Jagganath. The effigy of the deity was paraded on a large wheeled vehicle, under the wheels of which the deity's devotees are reputed to have voluntarily sacrificed themselves.

Justice of the Peace A magistrate appointed to hear minor cases, particularly in a small town or rural county. Justices of the Peace were not necessarily qualified in law, but were often recruited from the local gentry, and their appointment was signified on **calling cards** and other printed stationery by the use of the postnominal initials JP.

K

Kaffir A derogatory and racist term formerly used by **Boers** and other European settlers to describe indigenous peoples, particularly in Southern Africa. The terms Kaffirland or British Kaffirland were occasionally deployed when referring to the tribal territories of the Nguni and Xhosa peoples on the eastern coast of Southern Africa.

khaki A brownish-grey or dust-coloured cloth utilised for British military uniforms in both India and Southern Africa in the 1850s as a replacement for the conspicuous red jackets traditionally worn by foot regiments as late as the 1839 conflict in **Afghanistan**. The general election of 1900 was known as the 'Khaki Election' because of its association with the **Boer War** of 1899–1902.

Khyber Pass The most northerly and strategically important of the mountain passes in **Afghanistan** through which an incursion might be made into British-controlled India near the important centre of Peshawar. British forces engaged in hostilities with Afghan tribesmen in 1839, 1879 and 1897, with control of the pass being attained and lost several times

Kilmainham Treaty Not a legal treaty as such, but an informal agreement reached in May 1882 between the **Liberal Party** statesman William Ewart Gladstone (1809–98) and the Irish nationalist leader Charles Stewart Parnell (1846–91) which temporarily eased the ongoing deadlock between the British government and the **Irish National Land League**. The agreement, accounts of which were coloured by rumour and misinformation, was reported extensively in *Hansard* across May and June 1882.

Kirk, the The traditional name for the **Protestant** Church of Scotland. The Kirk is a Presbyterian denomination which, unlike the **Anglican** or other Episcopalian churches, does not recognise the ecclesiastical primacy of bishops or archbishops. Significant power is thus held by local congregations, particularly with regard to the appointment of ministers.

knacker A dealer in horseflesh, used as fresh food for cats and dogs, and in hooves, which were boiled down for glue. Knackers usually slaughtered the horses they purchased on their own premises, and the unregulated disposal of waste materials was on occasion associated with the contamination of domestic water supplies.

Kodak First marketed in the United States in 1888, the portable Kodak camera, which used a roll of flexible film rather than a glass plate to record the image in negative form, made amateur photography a possibility. The name was used generically in the Britain for both the original and derivative photographic devices.

kopje Sometimes anglicised as 'kop', a **Boer** word signifying a hill or high point.

L

Labouchère Amendment An amended provision of the 1885 *Criminal Law Amendment Act* (<u>48 & 49 Vict. c. 69</u>), introduced by the **Liberal Party** MP Henry Labouchère (1831–1912) which effectively declared all **homosexual** acts instances of 'gross indecency', whether undertaken in public or private, and even if sodomy was not actually practised.

Lady Margaret Hall An Anglican residential and educational establishment for female students within the University of Oxford, proposed in 1878 and opened in 1879. See also: **clubs; Somerville College.**

lancet A pointed blade, used in surgery. The name was adopted as the title of the most influential British medical periodical, founded in 1823. In architecture, a lancet is a narrow and pointed arch.

language of flowers (floriography) A convention in middle-class social intercourse in which various flowers were given a set of conventional associations, so that feelings and intentions could be conveyed wordlessly between, for example, lovers or friends. The practice was popularised through books such as *The Language of Flowers* (1884) with illustrations by Kate Greenaway (1846–1901).

lantern jaw A long countenance with a projecting lower jaw, the concave cheeks conventionally conveying a gaunt appearance.

Figure 18 'The Language of Flowers', British post-card issued by Regent Publishing Company (undated).

lawn tennis A racket sport played outdoors on a rectangular grass court. The rules of the British version of the game were formally codified in 1873 and revised in 1880 as tennis moved away from its earlier associations with **croquet** and royal tennis.

laudanum A bitter-tasting and reddish-coloured tincture of **opium** macerated in high-strength alcohol, used as an analgesic and on occasion as a recreational drug. Cheap and widely available for much of the century, its distribution was eventually restricted to trained dispensing chemists by the *Pharmacy Act* of 1868 (**31 & 32 Vict. c. 121**).

lead coffin A container of soldered lead, inserted within the wooden outer coffin or shell, in which a cadaver was placed immediately prior to burial. The sealed nature of the lead coffin preserves the dead body for a longer period of time while inhibiting the leakage of odours or bodily fluids. See also: **funeral**.

leaseholder An individual who retains the right to occupy or exploit a property under a contract with the actual owner, usually in consideration of a regular payment of rent in cash or by a share of profits or goods derived from the property. A leasehold property might be held for a considerable period by a leaseholder or their legal successor – leases of 99 years were not uncommon – though many were renewed annually. Leases and tenancies were conventionally renewed on one of the **quarter days**.

levee A formal reception, conventionally held in the early afternoon, presided over by the monarch, a senior member of the royal household or a **viceroy**, and attended by dignitaries, politicians and military or naval officers. In British Victorian practice, levees customarily excluded women from attendance.

Liberal Party The effective successor of the earlier **Whig** tendency in British politics, the Victorian Liberal Party was established in London on 6 June 1859, and under the dominant presence of William Ewart Gladstone influenced British and colonial politics until internal divisions over Irish **Home Rule** in 1886 split the party irrevocably. British Liberalism was influenced by **radicalism** and religious **nonconformity**, its leadership proposing many of the most significant political changes of the period, including reform of both the franchise and taxation and the **disestablishment** of the **Anglican** Church in Ireland. See also: **Conservative Party**; **Liberal Unionist**; **Tory**.

Liberal Unionist A faction of the **Liberal Party** which supported the **Conservative Party** in opposition to Irish **Home Rule** after 1886.

libraries See: **Carnegie libraries**; **circulating libraries**; **Mudie's**.

life-preserver A short club or truncheon, often weighted with lead, used in self-defence or as an offensive weapon.

Limehouse A district of East London with both a significant working-class population and, in the nineteenth century, a sizeable Chinese community. On account of the latter, the area became a byword in popular culture for unregulated gambling and **opium** dens.

limelight A reliable light source, produced by the burning of quicklime (calcium oxide), which progressively replaced the use of oil lamps in theatres and **music halls** from 1837.

livery The distinctive clothing worn by a domestic **servant**. On ceremonial occasions, and in grander domestic establishments, this might include a bicorn hat and gold-braided jacket, worn with breeches and silk stockings by **footmen** and carriage servants.

living in sin A moralistic euphemism for cohabitation outside of marriage, in popular use from at least the 1830s.

lock hospital A medical establishment which specialised in the treatment of **venereal diseases**. The moral imperative of such institutions frequently applied a greater burden of blame to women infected with **syphilis** than to their male counterparts.

Lombard Street A thoroughfare in the City of London associated with banking, insurance and finance generally.

London Gazette An official periodical in which statutory (that is, legally required) announcements are published. **Bankruptcies**, in particular, are announced in its pages.

London season The cycle of social events, such as balls, parties, formal visits and the presentation of **debutantes** to the reigning monarch at Court, which conventionally functioned also as a backdrop to introductions, courtship and marriage. The opening and closing of the Season, as it was usually known, varied each year, though a central event was invariably **Queen Charlotte's Ball**.

lorgnette A pair of spectacles fitted with a long handle which is held in front of the face rather than being worn on the nose. See also: **pince-nez**.

low church The **evangelical** wing of the **Anglican** Church, which characteristically favoured unadorned preaching in preference to **high-church** or **Anglo-Catholic** ceremonial.

low comedy A form of stage drama calculated to primarily amuse its audience rather than to convey any specific moral or political message. In the short form of the comic sketch, it was a staple component of **music-hall** entertainment.

Lowther Arcade A London shopping **arcade** constructed on The Strand in 1830, and by the mid-nineteenth century almost totally given over to the sale of children's toys. Part of the arcade was at one time occupied by the Royal Adelaide Gallery which hosted ostensibly educational lectures and exhibitions. Lowther Arcade was demolished in 1904.

Lucifer An early type of friction match, based upon the chemical phosphorus. White (sometimes called yellow) phosphorus is highly poisonous, and many of the – usually female – employees engaged in the manufacture of Lucifer matches suffered from degenerate physical conditions known as phossy jaw and Lucifer tongue, the containment of which necessitated radical surgery.

Luddites An oath-bound proletarian society of weavers and textile workers who took direct and violent action against the progressive mechanisation of the British cloth industry between 1811 and 1813. Acts of machine breaking and factory burning provoked the government to take firm military action, and many of those convicted were sentenced to **transportation** to Australia.

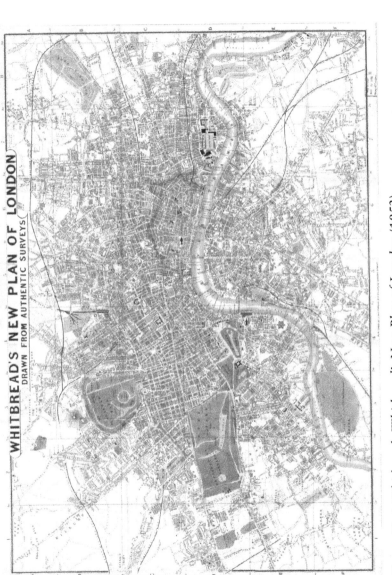

Figure 19 J. Whitbread, *Whitbread's New Plan of London* (1853).

lunacy Following centuries of unregulated containment within, variously, charitable or penal institutions, the insane were placed under the nominally curative care of local governance in the nineteenth century. The 1808 *County Asylums Act* (48 Geo. 3, c.96) encouraged **Justices of the Peace** to build local institutions to house pauper lunatics, the *Lunacy Act* of 1845 (8 & 9 Vict., c. 100) and a second *County Asylums Act* (8 and 9 Vict., c.126) in the same year further strengthening its provisions. Private lunatic asylums catered for wealthier families and gained a popular reputation for their supposed role in dispossessing or silencing middle- and upper-class women who resisted the patriarchal imperative of the family.

lying in A pre-Victorian euphemism for childbirth used across the nineteenth century. A lying-in hospital was, in essence, an establishment which dealt primarily with childbirth and addressed post-natal complications. Also known as: *accouchement*.

M

Madeira A fortified wine, popular in Britain, shipped from a Portuguese colony off the north-west coast of Africa. As was the case with **port**, the blending and shipping houses were sometimes managed or owned by British companies.

Maga See: *Blackwood's Edinburgh Magazine*.

magic lantern An early device for projecting static or moving images upon a wall or screen within a darkened room. Early magic lanterns were illuminated with candles or oil lamps, though later technology utilised gas jets and electric light bulbs. The slides which contained the images were usually made of glass encased within a wooden frame.

magistrate In the British legal system, a judge who presides over a court that has no jury and which considers for the most part only minor misdemeanours. Magistrates traditionally pass more serious offences (such as murder, robbery or sexual assaults) to a higher court, but pass sentence upon those convicted for offences such as common assault, criminal damage or burglary.

maharaja Derived from a Sanskrit word, the title of a high-ranking individual such as, in India particularly, a prince or ruler.

maid of all work A female **servant** whose duties included the whole range of household duties from domestic cleaning to the washing of clothes and linen and, in some cases, the cooking and serving of meals. Typically, a maid of all work would be employed in a modest household, and would most likely be the only servant.

majority, age of legal The age at which an individual was considered legally independent of their parent or guardian and thus able to enter into contracts and agreements on their own behalf, and to marry without parental consent. In Britain, the age of majority was set at twenty-one years until 1969. See also: **consent, age of.**

Manchester School A politically liberal movement, originating in Manchester around 1820, which advocated opposition to the **Corn Laws,** supported **Free Trade** and the campaign against **slavery,** as well as **disestablishment** in the form of the separation of the Church from the State.

man-eater A tiger, lion or other big cat which, having once killed a person, was assumed to hunt human flesh in preference to all other meats. Also used colloquially in reference to a woman with a reputation for sexual intrigues.

mantilla A scarf, often made of lace, worn by women over the head and shoulders as a fashion accessory. See also: **mantle.**

mantle A loose, sleeveless cloak or shawl worn by women.

mantrap A spring-loaded device, often employed in securing rural premises against the actions of poachers or trespassers. The mantrap would usually be concealed in undergrowth, and when stepped upon restrained the trespasser by the ankle. The powerful nature of the spring often caused injury, and the device could also be triggered by animals or children. The use of mantraps was restricted by the *Offences Against the Person Act* (<u>24 & 25 Vict. c. 100</u>) of 1861. See also: **field sports.**

marker An employee who attends upon **billiards** or **snooker** players, records the scores, and who might also be called upon to play a game against an unpartnered individual.

marking ink An indelible pigment commonly employed when writing the name of an individual upon garments that might customarily be sent to a public or communal laundry.

Married Women's Property Acts A term which covers two crucial parliamentary acts passed in 1870 (<u>33 & 34 Vict. c. 93</u>) and 1882 (<u>45 & 46 Vict. c.75</u>), and which may be applied also to separate legislation passed in India in 1874 (Act no. III of 1874. [24 February 1874]). The 1870 and 1882 acts formalised the relationship between a married woman and her personal assets which, historically in British practice, were ceded to the ownership and control of her husband upon marriage.

Marshalsea Prison A gaol located in Southwark, London, which specialised in the imprisonment of debtors and Admiralty prisoners such as smugglers, those charged with excise offences, and court-martialled sailors. It was closed in 1842.

matins A Christian service of morning prayer without any celebration of the **Eucharist**. See also: **evensong**.

Mauchline ware Any one of a variety of wooden trinkets, such as small boxes, cigar cases, tea caddies and needlework accessories, usually decorated with Scottish scenes and manufactured in Ayrshire, Scotland. See also: **Tartanware**.

Maxim gun An early machine gun invented by Sir Hiram Maxim in 1884.

meat safe Prior to the invention of domestic refrigeration, a mesh-sided box used to store meat at an ambient temperature and to protect it from flies and other parasites.

mechanics' institutes Educational establishments which, from the 1820s, supported the education and betterment of artisans and tradespeople, particularly in towns and cities. Known also by variety of other names – such as literary and scientific institutions, reading rooms, useful knowledge societies, athenaeums and lyceums – these local organisations often provided library facilities and hosted visiting speakers in sometimes substantial premises.

medium An individual purporting to act as a conduit between the dead and the living at a spiritualist **séance**. Mediums were essentially self-employed and often women, institutional **Spiritualism** being notably tolerant of female leadership when compared to the mainstream Christian churches.

meerschaum A term often applied to **tobacco** pipes manufactured from a type of porous mineral in order to distinguish them from the more common **briar** (or wooden) smoking implements.

melodrama A popular form of drama usually associated with sensational action and accompanied by music which both emphasises the mood of each scene and conceals the movement of scenery and stage machinery. The phrase is also applied to a tradition in prose fiction which anticipates the **sensation novel** in its interposition of scandalous situations upon the context of respectable family life.

memsahib A term applied, either as a description or else as a form of address, to a respectable white woman in colonial context. See also: **bwana**; **sahib**.

mens sana in corpore sano A Latin phrase denoting 'a healthy mind in a healthy body', used as a conventional description of the holistic aspirations of the British **public school** system. The education of boys within such establishments was prototypically premised upon an intellectual education in Classical culture supplemented by a regime of strenuous exercise, this latter being considered as contributing to a healthy morality. The public-school model was applied to British state education well into the twentieth century.

mercerised cotton Mercerisation is a textile-finishing treatment developed around 1844 and refined in 1890, which adds both tensile strength and a characteristic silky sheen to materials such as cotton.

mercury A highly poisonous chemical element which, nonetheless, was frequently prescribed in the nineteenth century as an antidote to **syphilis**. Administered as an ointment or ingested in the form of tablets, mercury suppressed some of the visible symptoms of syphilis though its continued administration was likely to prove fatal to the patient.

mesmerism A precursor to the **hypnotism** of the later century, mesmerism was claimed by some sincere medical practitioners as a diagnostic and therapeutic tool and deployed by many less-ethical individuals as a quack remedy supposedly capable of alleviating physiological discomfort or pain. Though a London Mesmeric Infirmary was opened in 1850, the development of chemical **anaesthesia** undermined the appeal of the pseudoscience, and by the **fin de siècle** it was evoked primarily as a plot device in **melodrama**, the **Gothic novel** and other genres of popular fiction.

Methodism A **Protestant** evangelical sect which legally separated from the **Anglican** Church in 1784, the Methodist Church eschewed the rigid and class-based hierarchical structure of the Church of England, attracting in consequence a significant following among the middle and working classes. Methodism became popularly associated with the **temperance movement** in the nineteenth century, opposed **slavery** and engaged with other social justice issues in Britain and abroad.

MFH The post-nominal letters which indicate that the possessor is a Master of Foxhounds, being either the owner of a pack of hounds used for **hunting** or the effective leader of the hunt in question.

midshipman In British naval usage, a junior officer undergoing training on a warship often in preparation for a lifelong career at sea.

militia A part-time and voluntary force of military personnel which was, historically, organised and recruited within county boundaries. From 1881 militia regiments were attached to units of the regular army and took on the name of these regiments. They were organised into the Special Reserve – the forerunner of the Territorial Army (now the Army Reserve) – in 1908.

millinery The manufacture and decorating of hats and similar headgear. The profession was notably gendered, with women's hats being crafted and adorned with feathers and other decorations mostly by female artisans, while the sturdier gentlemen's headgear (which often afforded an element of physical protection) was customarily constructed by a craftsman commonly termed a hatter rather than a milliner. See also: **billycock**; **coke hat**.

mob pistol Also known as a volley pistol, a firearm which possessed several barrels all of which could be fired simultaneously in an arc of discharge calculated to disable more than one assailant.

monthly nurse A nurse, not necessarily possessing a formal medical qualification, who attends a mother in the period immediately following childbirth.

moral management Part of the treatment and containment of lunacy, moral management was developed from the late eighteenth century and emphasised a humane approach to the mentally ill as opposed to the technologies of restraint which were in common use. Ideas and techniques pioneered at the York Retreat, a Quaker asylum founded in 1796, influenced the design of lunatic asylums, particularly by granting inmates ready access to fresh air and outdoor exercise, and discouraged the use of restraining furniture and punitive treatment.

mourning A formal period in which behaviour and dress are customarily modified as a response to the death of a parent, partner, child or other close associate. In Victorian Britain, mourning was a heavily codified process, though the rules were significantly gendered. A widow was expected to wear mourning clothing for at least two years following her bereavement, though the second might be taken as **half mourning**, where the uncompromisingly black **widow's weeds** of **full mourning** might be mitigated slightly with sombre shades of grey and purple. A widower observed a similar period of deep mourning, though its severity and extent might be tempered by the demands of his professional life. A father, mother, sibling or child was customarily mourned for a year, and more distant relations for between six and nine months. These distinctions, though, were most acutely observed in wealthier households, where the reclusive nature of mourning could be pursued without fear of significant financial hardship. Though often elaborate, particularly around the time of the interment, working-class mourning was invariably curtailed by the need to maintain dependants and often to recoup the outlay that funded an ostentatious **funeral**.

mourning band A strip of black **crepe**, worn around a hat or on the sleeve of a coat, as a public sign of respect following a bereavement. The depth of the band indicated the relative closeness of the mourner to the deceased, a wider **mourning** band being reserved for close relatives.

mourning jewellery The dead were frequently commemorated by items of memorial jewellery which could be worn long after the distinctive clothing of **mourning** was discarded. These mementoes included memorial rings, lockets and brooches which often embodied either a portrait or cameo of the deceased, or possibly a preserved lock of their hair. For gentlemen, perhaps the most extreme memento would be an **albert** supposedly crafted from the plaited hair of the deceased.

mourning stationery During the formal period of **mourning**, letters and other communications would customarily be sent out from wealthier households on paper bordered with black, and in envelopes which were similarly distinguished. As the period of mourning drew towards its close, the breadth of the border would be decreased incrementally. Those attending funerals were often presented with mourning cards, on which would be printed the name and significant dates of the deceased, the number and location of the grave and a suitable Bible verse. These were sometimes framed and displayed as a memento.

mourning warehouse Effectively, a form of department store which supplied the many components necessary for the elaborate process that was Victorian **mourning**. Regent Street institutions such as Jay's London General Mourning Warehouse, established in 1841, and Peter Robinson's Family Mourning Warehouse, opened in 1840, supplied **crepe** and cloth suitable for the manufacture of funeral garments, manufactured and sold clothing and headgear, and arranged funerals in the capacity of an **undertaker**.

moustache cup A drinking vessel incorporating a projecting inner lip which prevented the hot drink from touching (and thereby disturbing the shape and rigidity of) a gentleman's waxed moustache.

Mrs Beeton A colloquial and widespread contraction of the title of the most widely distributed domestic manual of the nineteenth century, *Beeton's Book of Household Management*, edited by Isabella Beeton (1836–65), and first published in 1861. As its full title suggests, Beeton's volume comprises far more than a mere collection of recipes or menus. The title page of the first edition, which was published by Beeton's publisher husband, markets the volume also to domestic **servants** from the **butler** and cook to the **valet** and **maid of all work**, while advising that its contents embrace 'sanitary, medical & legal memoranda'. As an index of the breadth of Victorian social attitudes and expectations, it is an essential resource.

Mrs Grundy A frequently cited – but wholly fictional – arbiter of domestic convention or social decorum. Mrs Grundy was originally an unseen character in Thomas Morton's 1798 drama *Speed the Plough* but became a touchstone of sufficient weight to be alluded to in Dickens's *Hard Times* (1854) and Thackeray's *Vanity Fair* (1847–8).

Mudie's In full, Mudie's Select Library, the most prominent of the Victorian **circulating libraries** and a major commercial purchaser of books in the age of the **triple-decker** novel.

mudlark An individual who searches the muddy banks of a river in the hope of finding coins, scrap metal or other discarded items.

muffin A flat and usually circular form of bread which is split, toasted and eaten hot with butter. The Victorian muffin does not resemble the cupcake muffin of the twenty-first century, and in grander houses was presented to diners in a covered container called a muffineer.

muffler A scarf worn round the throat or lower face for protection from cold or moisture, and sometimes to conceal identity also.

muscular Christianity A doctrine in masculine culture very much aligned to the tenets of *mens sana in coprore sano*, and popularly associated with the preaching of the **Anglican** cleric Charles Kingsley (1819–75) and the fiction of Thomas Hughes

(1822–96). Muscular Christians regarded vigorous exercise, team sports and physical service as a concrete expression of their faith, and conducive with the inculcation of personal chivalry and sound morals.

music hall A form of theatrical entertainment popular with working-class audiences in particular but attracting members of other social classes as well. Essentially a variety performance, it involved short comedic sketches, comic and pathetic songs, possibly a short **melodrama**, a pantomime or a farcical **low comedy**, sometimes a stage magician, contortionist or acrobat, and often an element of audience participation in the form of songs led from the stage. The regulations governing music halls were somewhat less stringent than those associated with theatre, and it is possibly for this reason that music-hall entertainment often touched suggestively on sexual topics such as seduction, pregnancy and adultery.

mute A professional mourner hired to attend a funeral. Mutes wore deep **mourning**, often supplemented by a crepe sash and a formal staff similarly draped in black material.

N

Naples biscuit A type of biscuit, flavoured with rosewater.

National Hunt Racing See: steeplechase.

National Vigilance Association Formed in 1885, an organisation which campaigned against public access to **pornography** and investigated the sexual abuses inherent in **prostitution**, particularly in the case of the procurement of children for sexual exploitation and the transportation of British girls and women to overseas brothels. Among the early members of the Association was W. T. Stead (1849–1912), editor of the *Pall Mall Gazette*. See also: **Society for the Suppression of Vice.**

nautch girl In Indian context, a professional female dancer who may also sing as part of her performance.

nem. con. In full, *nemine contradicente*, an abbreviation frequently encountered in written reports of debates and meetings which indicates that a motion or proposal has been passed without anybody speaking or voting against it.

neurasthenia A morbid condition of the nervous system, the characteristic symptoms of which included lassitude, headaches, muscular pain and – in some reported cases – subjective and temporary sensory disturbances. See also: **hysteria.**

Figure 20 The New Woman as literary intellectual: poster advertising an 1894 production at J. Comyns Carr's Comedy Theatre, Westminster.

New Woman A proto-feminist icon of the **fin de siècle**, the New Woman was arguably a more substantial figure than her close compatriot, the **Girl of the Period**. Associated particularly with sexual issues – characteristically, New Women aspired to financial independence outside of marriage and expressed a distaste for monogamy and wifely submission – the New Woman was feared and ridiculed by social commentators, journalists and fictionalists of both sexes. She was popularly derided as an overbearing intellectual, invading the masculine territory of the collegiate **university**; an enthusiastic participant in **field sports** such as **hunting** and **shooting**; a reckless cyclist, often dressed in a parody of the **Bloomer costume**; an inadequate wife failing to cater for her husband's needs and a neglectful mother to her children, these latter suggesting that her aspirations had somehow unsexed her and rendered her biologically 'unnatural'.

Newgate One of London's oldest gaols, Newgate was adjacent to the **Old Bailey** and was the location of **public executions** following the removal of the gallows from Tyburn. Public executions

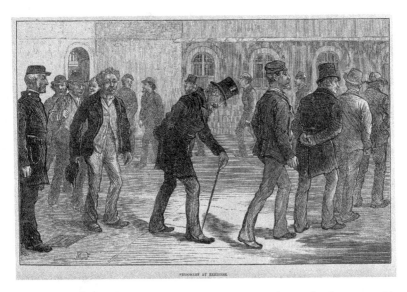

Figure 21 The exercise yard at Newgate Gaol. Michael Fitzgerald, 'Prisoners at Exercise', from 'Sketches in Newgate', *Illustrated London News*, 22 February 1873.

ceased in 1868, though Newgate continued to house and execute condemned felons until its closure in 1902.

Newnham College Opened as a residential house for five female students in 1871, the second exclusively female college within the University of Cambridge adopted a more 'gradualist' approach to the education of women than that associated with **Girton College**, in that it did not initially seek to integrate all of its students into the existing courses pursued by men. Female students at the university were permitted to enter examinations from 1881, but were not granted degrees until 1948. See also: **Clubs.**

night-soil man An individual employed to remove human excrement and other waste from lavatories (often known as privies or earth closets) each evening. See also: **dust.**

Nineteenth Century, The A monthly magazine founded by James Knowles (1831–1908) in 1877. The content was serious – science, religion, ethics, aesthetics – and the contributors included prominent politicians, clergymen and authors. The title was changed to

The Nineteenth Century and After in 1901, and to *The Twentieth Century* in 1951. It ceased publication in 1972.

Noah's Ark With its pairs of wooden animals, supported by human figures depicting Noah's family, this was in many cases the only toy a Victorian child might be allowed to play with on Sundays in religious households.

nonconformist A Protestant who is a member of a religious denomination other than that of the Established or **Anglican** Church. The expression of religious nonconformity, whether through large organisations such as the **Methodist** Church or the Baptist Union or in smaller and often local congregations, was often accompanied by a concern for social or moral issues including the abolition of **slavery, disestablishment, temperance** and political **radicalism.**

Norfolk jacket A loose-fitting gentleman's jacket with a waistband, originally a garment worn for **shooting** but adaptable also to angling and cycling. A Norfolk suit added knee-breeches to the jacket.

North-West Frontier The border between the British-controlled Punjab (now north-west Pakistan) and Afghanistan. Annexed by the **East India Company** following the Second Sikh War of 1848–9, the region was notoriously subject to intertribal conflict as well as local resistance to British rule.

Northwest Passage The sea route between the Atlantic and Pacific Oceans by way of the Arctic Ocean. Suitable routes were discovered by explorers in 1850 and 1854, though a successful navigation was only achieved in the first decade of the twentieth century.

O

oakum Fibres obtained by untwisting old hemp ropes, used for caulking (sealing) the wooden decks of ships and making watertight joints in pipes. Picking oakum – a laborious process which abraded the skin of the fingers – was often undertaken by prisoners within Victorian gaols as prescribed **hard labour.**

Oddfellows A fraternal organisation with antecedents in earlier trade guilds and an eighteenth-century benefit society, the Independent Order of Oddfellows Manchester Unity was founded in Salford in 1810. Organised in lodges on the model of **Freemasonry**, the Oddfellows enjoyed the royal patronage of William IV (1765–1837), becoming the largest and richest **friendly society** in the world by 1851. Female lodges were introduced in 1893, an equal membership status to that enjoyed by male Oddfellows being granted in 1898.

odyle Also known as odic force or od, a hypothetical natural force, pervasive and somewhat resembling the intangible fluid of **mesmerism**, variously associated with magnetism, electricity or the vital force of life itself as expressed through physical or psychological phenomena.

Old Bailey, the The central criminal court of London between 1674 and 1913. The original courthouse was located next to **Newgate Gaol** and within sight of St Paul's Cathedral.

omnibus A horse-drawn public conveyance, often with an upper deck, which followed a set route and charged a fixed rate for passengers over relatively short distances. The upper deck, where present, was often open to the elements and consequently attracted a lower fare. Identifiable omnibus services appear to have originated in urban Britain as early as 1824 (in Manchester) and in London in 1829, vehicles in the latter location being known for some time as Shillibeers in honour of their proprietor.

Representing the debilitated state of the body from the effects of onanism or Self-pollution.

Figure 22 The physical debilitation of the habitual masturbator. Plate 1 to R. J. Brodie, *The Secret Companion* (c. 1845).

onanism A euphemism for the supposedly injurious practice of masturbation. The term is an inaccurate allusion to Genesis 38: 8–9 which, strictly speaking, depicts an act of coitus interruptus. Popularly, the so-called 'secret vice' of onanism manifested itself upon the body, producing a variety of well-known physiological symptoms including clammy and pallid skin, deficient eyesight, hairy palms and bad breath as well as a languorous demeanour that was supposedly a consequence of a depleted circulation, semen being ostensibly a by-product of blood. The physical lassitude of the onanist was prototypically accompanied by a moral weakness: in both popular cultural mythology and **pornography**, onanists frequently initiated others into their ostensibly degrading vice as well as into active **homosexuality**. See also: **spermatic economy**.

open voting The practice of electing a candidate by way of a public show of hands, rather than in private by secret ballot. The public nature of elections rendered voters vulnerable to physical intimidation or threats of raised rents or other impositions where the candidate was a landlord or business associate, and was regarded by enthusiasts for **Home Rule** as being particularly acute in Ireland. The practice was abolished in 1872 by the *Ballot Act* (35 & 36 Vict. c. 33).

opera The early-century vogue for Italian operas gave way successively to the lighter and more accessible tradition of the **Savoy Opera** at mid-century, and latterly to the more expansive and grandiose production of works by Giuseppe Verdi (1813–1901) and Richard Wagner (1813–83). For those not necessarily familiar with the Italian or German languages, the attraction of opera was possibly less the storytelling and more the personal attractiveness of female sopranos such as Jenny Lind (1820–87), Adelina Patti (1843–1919) and Nellie Melba (1861–1931), the elaborate staging of later works – which often drew on lighting and stage technology pioneered by Henry Irving (1838–1905) at the Lyceum **Theatre** in London – and the opportunity to be numbered among, for example, a cultural elite such as the so-called Wagnerites.

opera glasses A small telescope or, more commonly, pair of fixed-focus binoculars, used by patrons during performances in theatres and opera houses.

opium The reddish-brown secretion of the opium poppy (*Papaver somniferum*), opium was a narcotic deployed both medicinally and recreationally across the century. It was a crucial ingredient in proprietary sleep-inducing preparations such as **black drop**, a common analgesic in the form of **laudanum** and, when smoked, a potent hallucinogen as well as a relaxant. Popular culture associates opium with China, and the recreational opium den with Chinese immigrants to Europe, though the drug was sourced also from India and Afghanistan. See also: **Opium Wars**.

Opium Wars Two wars fought between Britain and China between 1839 and 1842, and between an alliance of Britain and France, again against China, between 1856 and 1860 for control of the lucrative opium trade. Conflict was initiated not to control opium exports *from* China but, rather, to maintain the largely illegal import of Indian opium *into* that country, though other ostensible disputes (such as the mistreatment or murder of British or French citizens or damage to foreign-owned cargoes or factories by Chinese officials) were also cited as justification for naval and military intervention. Chinese defeat in both Opium Wars led to trading and territorial concessions in favour of the victors, including the ceding of Hong Kong Island to the British in 1842.

Orangeman A member of a fraternal Protestant society founded in Ireland in 1795. The Orange Order spread across the British Empire during the nineteenth century, often following the movement of military regiments, with Orange lodges being formed in Australia, Canada, Hong Kong, New Zealand and Southern Africa. In Britain, the Orange Order was instrumental in opposing such national political ventures as **Catholic emancipation** and **Home Rule**, as well as countering what was perceived to be the enhanced influence of **Roman Catholicism** in local government, educational policy and **Anglican** ritual. Though strongest as a political and cultural force in Ireland, Orangeism was nonetheless a significant presence in Victorian Scotland and England, with Glasgow, Liverpool and Manchester being particular centres for the movement.

organza Thin and stiff fabric for dresses, often made of silk.

ostler A **servant** who attends to horses, particularly one employed at an inn or hotel. The equivalent servant in a domestic household is usually termed a **groom**.

outdoor relief Maintenance, in the form of cash, food or occasionally clothing, granted to paupers not resident in a **workhouse** under the unreformed **Poor Law**. Outdoor relief was regarded by many of those whose finances underwrote the local administration of the Poor Law as a tacit encouragement for the able-bodied poor to avoid work and produce children whom they could not afford to keep – a particular moral distaste being reserved for **illegitimacy**. Legislation in 1832 restricted the distribution of outdoor relief to the able-bodied, associating it with hard physical work such as **oakum** picking or **stone-breaking,** and its administration to all able-bodied individuals was ostensibly ended by the *Order Prohibiting Outdoor Relief* of 1844, though many local Poor Law Unions continued to administer the benefit following this legislation. See also: **indoor relief.**

Oxford Movement A **high-church** tendency within the **Anglican** communion, the name acknowledging its philosophical origins within the colleges of the University of Oxford. Also known as Tractarians, following the publication of a series of doctrinal *Tracts for the Times* between 1833 and 1841, adherents of the movement challenged the **Protestant** and **evangelical** traditions of the Church of England, and proposed fundamental changes to its theology and liturgy clearly influenced by **Roman Catholicism**. Frustrated by conservative bishops and restricted in some cases by litigation invoking **canon law,** some Tractarians turned to Anglo-Catholic missionary work in the urban slums of Britain while others converted to Roman Catholicism.

P

packet boat A vessel which travels according to a timetable between two ports, carrying mail and in many cases passengers also.

Paddy Also known as Pat, a personification of Ireland in masculine guise. The stereotype as depicted in English cartoons, such as those in *Punch*, was overwhelmingly derogatory, the expression of the face being variously savage or else stupid, and the garments a ragged imagination of peasant dress. Weapons were almost invariably associated with representations produced during periods of **Fenian** agitation. The personification of Ulster **Protestants** was somewhat more positive in British **Unionist** journals, and Nationalist periodicals produced in Ireland itself tended to a more positive vision of the rural Irish. See also: **John Bull**

pall A heavy cloth, often of dark-coloured velvet, which was draped over the coffin throughout its journey to the **funeral** service. While black and burgundy were common colours for adult **mourning**, white was sometimes utilised to signify the interment of a child or an unmarried woman. The men employed by the **undertaker** to carry the coffin from hearse to church or **chapel** were termed 'pallbearers'.

Pall Mall Gazette A London daily newspaper published between 1865 and 1923, the *Pall Mall Gazette* gained particular notoriety for its 1885 exposure of child prostitution and the exploitation of girls under the **age of consent**, 'The Maiden Tribute of Modern Babylon', by its editor W. T. Stead (1849–1912).

pantechnicon A building which houses a large collection of shops or stalls, particularly those dealing in exotic goods. The term may also be applied to a large horse-drawn vehicle, suitable for the movement of furniture.

papal aggression The popular term for the actions of Pope Pius IX (1792–1878) who, in 1850, re-established a **Roman Catholic** hierarchy within England of thirteen bishops under an Archbishop of Westminster. This act, which was viewed by many **Protestants** as an affront to **Anglican** ascendancy and governance, provoked further the existing **low-church** antipathy towards ritualism and the **Oxford Movement** to the extent that some **high-church** services were disrupted by protestors.

papal infallibility The **Roman Catholic** doctrine that the pope, when speaking *ex cathedra* (that is, in his capacity as *Pontifex Maximus*, or Supreme Pontiff), cannot be capable of error when he defines the Church's position on a matter of faith or morals. When formally proclaimed by Pope Pius IX (1792–1878) in 1870, this dogma provoked a degree of **Protestant** outrage in its implicit assumption of a form of control over *all* Christians. William Ewart Gladstone (1809–98), nominally one of the most tolerant of statesmen to address the competing politics of Church and State, was among the most vitriolic of respondents to the claim of the papacy, his pamphlet *The Vatican Degrees in their Bearing on Civil Allegiance* (1874) succinctly outlining his objections.

paper duty A tax on paper which was removed through being included in the 1861 Budget tabled by the **Liberal** Chancellor of the Exchequer William Ewart Gladstone (1809–98). The reduction in the price of paper further reduced the cost of newsprint, as well as making politically radical publication and pamphleteering both cheaper and easier. See also: **stamp duty**.

parish The **Anglican** Church was historically administered by dividing up both rural and urban areas into parishes, where the ministry of the clergy was supported by appointed or elected individuals who oversaw the distribution of charity, the welfare of the sick and the maintenance of local facilities. These often ancient demarcations were adopted as the basis for later secular and civil administration, and in consequence underwrote both formal and informal local identities and affiliations.

parson A **Protestant** clergyman, particularly a member of the **Anglican** Church.

patent medicine A proprietary medicine which may be obtained without a formal prescription. Victorian patent medicines were notorious for the extravagance of their curative claims, though a degree of euphemism was employed when marketing abortifacients to women and ostensible 'cures' for **syphilis** to both sexes. Some patent medicines were relatively harmless and quite possibly derived from traditional folk remedies; others, though, were **adulterated** with injurious substances such as **mercury**, lead and copper as well as more potent ingredients including, commonly, **opium**.

pawnbroker An individual or company which lends money on the security of an article deposited ('pawned') for the period of the loan. In working-class districts, pawnbrokering was a largely unregulated and essential form of usury, with pawnbrokers lending money, for comparatively short periods of time and at often high rates of interest, on the security of items such as clothing, tools and furniture. See also: **gombeenism**.

Peabody Trust Founded by a wealthy American, George Peabody (1795–1869), an organisation which developed what would today be known as social housing – basically, affordable and hygienic rented accommodation – for the working classes in London.

pea-souper A dense, often yellow-tinged fog characteristic of urban pollution. The term appears to have originated in the 1890s.

peeler A colloquial term for a **police** officer, derived from the name of Sir Robert Peel (1788–1850), who established the Metropolitan Police in London in 1829.

peerage The collective term for those citizens who possess a legal title, and possibly lands and civil privileges also, on an hereditary basis. In Victorian Britain, many peers enjoyed the right to sit without election in the legislative **House of Lords**, and an established ritual of precedence and ceremonial governed how they were formally received and greeted at public and private events. Individuals who are not peers are officially termed 'commoners'. The highest hereditary rank in the peerage is that of duke, followed by marquess, earl, viscount and baron. **Baronets** are not peers, even where their status has been granted through inheritance. Broadly speaking, English and Scottish peers precede Irish peers, though many peers hold titles in more than one country.

penal servitude Following the abolition of **transportation** in 1853, felons who might previously have been sent to Australia were sentenced to a penal servitude comprising domestic imprisonment with compulsory **hard labour** (such as working a **treadmill** or picking **oakum**).

penknife A small and sharp blade originally employed in the cutting of quill pens. The introduction of mass-produced metal nibs in the late 1820s made the actual name of the implement an anachronism, though its utility in everyday life ensured its survival.

Penny Black The first printed postage stamp issued by the Post Office on 6 May 1840. Prior to this development, the penny post (which carried mail at a fixed fee between postal towns) marked letters with inked impressions to signify due receipt of payment.

penny dreadful A cheaply published story, usually **melodramatic** in nature and premised upon themes of crime or horror. The genre emerged in the 1830s and was probably at its peak in the 1860s and 1870s. Popular themes included narratives of celebrated and semi-mythological criminals such as Dick Turpin or Charles Peace, tales of depravity in urban London such as *Sweeney Todd, The Demon Barber of Fleet Street* and more overt Gothic works concerning **Spring-Heeled Jack** or – in long-running serial form – *Varney the Vampyre*.

penny farthing A velocipede or **bicycle** with a large front wheel and a smaller trailing wheel (the name comparing these to the comparative size of two British coins), in which the front (and steering) wheel is driven directly by pedals rather than through a chain and gears. Probably invented in France in the 1860s, it was developed and manufactured in Britain from around 1870.

penny gaff A cheap place of amusement, such as a **music hall** or a low-class theatre.

People's Charter See: Chartism.

Figure 23 The Penny Black postage stamp of 1840.

pepper and salt A type of cloth made of alternating light and dark threads which gives an overall grey appearance from a distance. Material of this type was often used in the manufacture of gentlemen's jackets, trousers and overcoats.

Peter Parley's Magazine An English periodical published between 1839 and 1863 which published short fiction, poetry and factual articles for younger readers.

Peterloo A violent encounter in St Peter's Field, Manchester, on 16 August 1819 between, on the one side, primarily working-class **radicals** gathered to hear speeches by, among others, the celebrated 'Orator' Henry Hunt (1773–1835) and, on the other, members of the regular army, the local yeomanry (essentially a paramilitary force) and special constables. Alarmed at the presence of a crowd which may have numbered as many as 60,000, local magistrates read the **Riot Act** to the protestors, before the troops – which included cavalry – attempted to arrest the speakers and disperse the crowd using lethal force. An estimated eighteen people, including four women and a child, died and there were over 700 recorded injuries. The name Peterloo was coined a few days after the massacre as an ironic reminder of the perceived heroism of the military at Waterloo, and reportage of the event did much to enhance public consciousness of the restricted nature of the suffrage in urban and working-class areas.

Petticoat Lane Now known as Middlesex Street, the centre of a district in working-class east London which housed an unregulated market, a number of **pawnbrokers** and receivers of stolen goods, and a large Jewish community whose numbers were swelled by immigrants following the European pogroms of the fin de siècle.

pheasant shooting A **field sport** in which birds are 'beaten' – that is, disturbed from their hiding places in the undergrowth by 'beaters' – and then despatched with a shotgun by participants. Shooting parties formed a major component of country-house weekends, these being occasions not merely for sport but also business encounters and romantic matchmaking. The shooting season in England runs from 1 October to 1 February annually, though it is illegal to take **game** on Sundays and on Christmas Day.

Phoenix Park Murders See: Invincibles.

phonograph A forerunner of the gramophone invented in 1877 and improved in the 1880s, this clockwork-powered device enabled the production of relatively faithful recordings of the human voice and other sounds on a wax-coated cylinder.

photography Photographic images were produced using rudimentary cameras and chemically infused surfaces such as stone, metal and, more commonly, glass – as early as the 1820s. The development of portable cameras and the commercial possibilities afforded by travelling and high-street photographic studios popularised photography as a medium, albeit one still requiring both fragile glass plates and long exposure times for each monochrome image. The **Kodak** camera, introduced in 1888, led to amateur photography becoming a mass hobby, in part because the image was developed by the manufacturer rather than the photographer. See also: **spirit photography**.

phrenology A pseudoscience introduced to Britain from the European continent in the early nineteenth century, phrenology – also known as craniology and cranioscopy – mapped perceived human character onto a series of 'organs' whose locations were supposedly identifiable on the surface of the skull. Excess in an emotion or character trait was indicated customarily by a raised cranial contour, deficiency by absence of the same. Phrenology

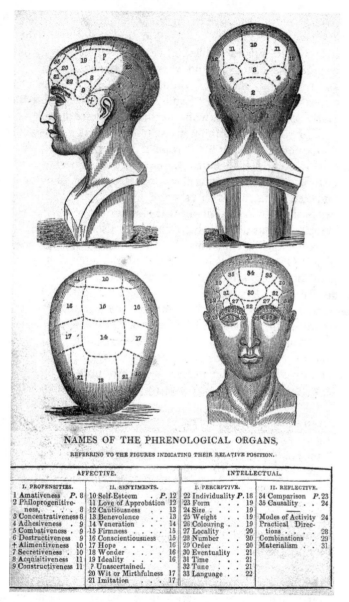

NAMES OF THE PHRENOLOGICAL ORGANS,

REFERRING TO THE FIGURES INDICATING THEIR RELATIVE POSITION.

AFFECTIVE.		INTELLECTUAL.	
I. PROPENSITIES.	II. SENTIMENTS.	I. PERCEPTIVE.	II. REFLECTIVE.
1 Amativeness *P.* 8	10 Self-Esteem . *P.* 12	22 Individuality *P.* 18	34 Comparison *P.* 23
2 Philoprogenitive-	11 Love of Approbation 12	23 Form 19	35 Causality . . 24
ness, . . . 8	12 Cautiousness . . 13	24 Size 19	
3 Concentrativeness 8	13 Benevolence . . 13	25 Weight . . . 19	Modes of Activity 24
4 Adhesiveness . 9	14 Veneration . . 14	26 Colouring . . 19	Practical Direc-
5 Combativeness . 9	15 Firmness 15	27 Locality . . 20	tions 28
6 Destructiveness . 9	16 Conscientiousness . 15	28 Number . . . 20	Combinations . . 29
† Alimentiveness 10	17 Hope 16	29 Order . . . 20	Materialism . . 31
7 Secretiveness . 10	18 Wonder 16	30 Eventuality . . 21	
8 Acquisitiveness 11	19 Ideality . . . 16	31 Time . . . 21	
9 Constructiveness 11	? Unascertained.	32 Tune . . . 21	
	20 Wit or Mirthfulness 17	33 Language . . 22	
	21 Imitation . . . 17		

Figure 24 One of the earliest systematic charts of the phrenological organs as understood in Britain immediately prior to the coronation of Queen Victoria. Frontispiece to George Combe, *Outlines of Phrenology* (1836).

was popularised in Britain through a network of local societies which organised lectures and demonstrations and exhibited skulls and casts of celebrity crania, the chief spokesman for the movement being the Scot George Combe (1788–1858). After Combe's death, phrenology became increasingly disorganised as a movement, with the American entrepreneur Lorenzo Fowler (1811–96) coming to dominate its survival in the later nineteenth century through the marketing of mass-produced phrenological busts and charts.

phthisis. A term used to describe pulmonary **tuberculosis** in both popular and medical works across the nineteenth century.

physician A medical professional who examines the body, makes diagnoses and prognoses, and prescribes medicines but who does *not* engage in interventive surgery. A physician-accoucheur would supervise childbirth at a lying-in hospital for wealthier patients, though the majority of births would have taken place in the domestic environment and under the supervision of a female midwife who, though often experienced, would not likely have received extensive clinical training. See also: **surgeon.**

physiognomy A pseudoscience which claimed that an individual's character and temperament might be accurately discerned from the conformation of their face, physiognomy was popularised in the late eighteenth century by Johann Kasper Lavater (1741–1801) and revived as **phrenology** extended its compass to the cranium as a whole. Writers of fiction commonly employed the conventions of popular physiognomy, as did those acting stage **melodrama.**

piecework Labour in which the employee is paid for the quantity of goods finished rather than by the number of hours worked.

piers Sometimes referred to as pleasure piers, these typically cast-iron and wood structures were a common feature of British seaside resorts from 1814 (when the first, Ryde Pier, was constructed). They provided, variously, a linear space for pedestrian promenading, often punctuated by novelty shops and catering establishments, a venue for theatrical and musical entertainments, and frequently a pier-head at which commercial steamers might dock. Llandudno Pier (opened 1878) is a representative example, albeit with some Edwardian modifications.

pigeoned To have been cheated or swindled.

pince-nez Spectacles which are held in place by a flexible spring upon the bridge of the nose, rather than by arms attached to the frame. See also: **lorgnette.**

pinchbeck An alloy of copper and zinc which, because of its resemblance to gold, is used in the manufacture of both cheap and counterfeit jewellery.

pith helmet See: sola topee.

planchette A small board, mounted upon free-running castors, used in **spiritualism** as a supposed medium through which the dead may communicate with the living during a séance. The planchette was typically a pointing device through which a series of letters and numbers arranged around its perimeter might be indicated by the ostensible spirit, though a similar instrument incorporating a pen or pencil was sometimes used when attempting to obtain automatic or spirit writing. As the planchette was in effect always under the hand of the **medium**, and possibly of the sitters at the séance also, any messages it conveyed were always liable to allegations of human manipulation.

poaching See: game.

poet laureate A poet appointed nominally by the Crown, but usually following consultation with the government of the day, whose duties are to mark important national and royal events by tributes in verse. Prior to 1999, British poets laureate were appointed for life, and though part of their remuneration traditionally included an allocation of wine or sherry, this convention was not routinely adhered to in the nineteenth century. The poets laureate of Queen Victoria's reign were Robert Southey (in office 1813–43), William Wordsworth (1843–50), Alfred Tennyson (1850–92) and Alfred Austin (1896–1913).

police Though small-scale and specifically local policing had been in place in parts of England and Scotland prior to the nineteenth century, increased industrialisation and urbanisation prompted the formation of a significant new police forces – particularly in port cities such as Glasgow (1800) and Bristol (1803) – in the period leading up to the foundation of the Metropolitan Police in 1829. A local force was established in Belfast in 1816 and a larger Constabulary of Ireland in 1822 which became the Royal Irish Constabulary in 1867. British policing outside of Ireland was based historically upon local forces rather than a national constabulary, routinely patrolled without firearms, and was for the most part uniformed while in service. A Detective Branch, which operated on occasion in civilian dress, was opened by the

Metropolitan Police in 1842, and a **Special Branch** in 1883. See also: **Bow Street Runners; peeler.**

polo The conventions of modern polo can be dated to 1859 and the foundation of the Silchur Polo Club in Manipur, India, the British members of which set down formal rules for an ancient equestrian game which they had seen played by the indigenous population. Travelling with the army, polo reached England in 1869. Played in periods known as **chukkas,** teams of mounted payers attempt to score goals by hitting a hard ball with the side of a long-handled mallet.

pooh! An expression of contempt or disdain. To pooh-pooh is to dismiss an idea, subject or individual as nonsensical, irrelevant or unimportant. See also: **pshaw!**

pooh-bah Derived from the name of a character in *The Mikado* (1885), one of the **Savoy Operas,** a usually derogative term which is applied to an individual who either holds many offices or else aggrandises his own importance by behaving in a pompous and imperious manner

Poor Law The collective term for a complicated system of acts of Parliament, some of them ancient, by which those who were unable to work and had no means of subsistence were cared for on a local basis. A Royal Commission was appointed in 1832 in order to consider, revise and reform the existing legislation, and a *Poor Law Amendment Act* (4 & 5 Will. 4 c. 76) was passed by Parliament in 1834, with separate legislation being tabled for Scotland and Ireland. Under the 1834 act, a new Poor Law Commission was empowered to appoint inspectors who would oversee local implementation, and the administration of relief was removed from the control of **parishes** and passed to locally elected boards of guardians, each administering a **workhouse.** The 1834 act aimed to end the granting of **outdoor relief** to the able-bodied, though such assistance might be given to the sick or elderly.

popery A derogatory term employed to describe both the doctrines and the institution of the **Roman Catholic** Church. **Protestant** and **evangelical** distaste for the perceptibly 'popish' ceremonial practices favoured by the **Tractarians** and **Oxford Movement** was often expressed by a vehement application of the same terminology.

pornography Printed fiction, perhaps surprisingly, was often less attentively regulated than theatrical performance and, though the publishers of pornography might be prosecuted for outraging public morality or indecency under the 1857 *Obscene Publications Act* (20 & 21 Vict. c. 83), a sizeable body of erotica remained available to those purchasers aware of an essentially underground and euphemistic distribution network. Much of this material was privately printed, bearing no publisher's name on the title page, and a proportion originated in London's **Holywell Street**, a thoroughfare once associated with radical pamphleteering.

port A fortified red wine from Portugal, popular as a *digestif* following meals. The excessive consumption of port was popularly considered a cause of **gout**.

porter A dark and bitter beer brewed using charred malt.

postilion A term which may be applied, variously, to a despatch rider or post-boy who carries messages and packages, or to a mounted horseman who controls a coach or carriage when there is no coachman seated on the vehicle itself.

potato famine An extended period of famine and economic distress caused by a blight which destroyed both the leaves and the tubers of the potato crop. The Irish potato famine of 1845–52 was the most serious of several outbreaks across Europe, and in addition to causing the death of around 1 million inhabitants of Ireland through starvation and related causes, prompted the immigration of a similar number. The famine brought into sharp relief not merely the deficiencies and inequalities of the **Poor Law** systems of Ireland and England, but also the comparative underdevelopment of the economy of the island, which remained largely agricultural, and the danger of dependence upon a single arable crop.

praelector A fellow of a college within one of the Universities of Oxford or Cambridge. In the latter institution, a praelector is held vicariously responsible for a student's actions and may incur a personal punishment should a transgression be detected. See also: *in loco parentis*.

Pre-Raphaelites A brotherhood of artists, formed in London in 1849, whose paintings characteristically made bold use of colour and a degree of realism in representation, and often addressed matters of social concern (such as adultery, prostitution and inequality of wealth) as well as chivalric, religious and mythological subjects. The principal members were William Holman Hunt

(1827–1910), John Everett Millais (1829–96) and Dante Gabriel Rossetti (1828–82), the latter frequently imbricating his painting with poetry. The Pre-Raphaelite Brotherhood (abbreviated PRB) was an important context of the culture behind the **Arts and Crafts movement.**

press A cupboard such as might be used for the storage of clothes or household utensils.

Primrose League Founded in 1883, and named after the reputedly favourite flower of the **Tory** politician Benjamin Disraeli (1804–81), this mass organisation was premised upon the principles of the **Conservative Party**, and in particular its commitment to empire, national integrity and Christianity – avowed atheists were, notably, not considered eligible for membership. Utilising a national network of branches, publishing a regular journal, and employing an elaborate honours system of associates, knights and dames, membership of which was publicised through the wearing of emblems and ribbons, the League was noteworthy in facilitating the entry of women into extra-parliamentary politics on something approaching an equal footing with their male counterparts. The national membership of the Primrose League reputedly approached 1,000,000 by the **fin de siècle**, and though its influence and subscription base declined following the First World War, it was not formally dissolved until 2004.

prince consort The husband of a reigning queen who is not himself a king. Queen Victoria's husband, Prince Albert of Saxe-Coburg and Gotha (1819–61) – the son of a German duke – was created Prince Consort in 1857.

Prince of Wales A royal title, instituted in 1301, traditionally granted to the eldest son of the English and later British monarch, who is also heir apparent to the throne. The title was held by Prince Albert Edward (1841–1910), informally known as 'Bertie', from 1841 until his proclamation as King Edward VII in 1901.

prison hulk A decommissioned warship, used as a floating prison partially in response to a shortage of accommodation in conventional prisons. Hulks provided accommodation for convicts sentenced to **transportation** and awaiting transit on seaworthy vessels known as convict transports, though some prisoners might serve their whole sentence on a hulk. Prison hulks were moored at seaports across the United Kingdom, and also formed part of the punitive regime in the colonies, most notably Australia.

Figure 25 Albert Edward, Prince of Wales and heir to the throne, depicted as the Grand Master of English Freemasons (1874–1901).

problem play A play in which a social or cultural issue, particularly one attracting controversy, is dramatised and explored. The problem play reached its apex in British culture in the intellectual and moral debate surrounding the **fin de siècle** dramas of Henrik Ibsen (1828–1906), though many of the issues raised in his works – the inequalities of marriage, the stigma of illegitimacy or disease, and the debilitative consequences of moral hypocrisy – could be found in the low culture of **melodrama**.

proctor At the Universities of Oxford and Cambridge, an official whose duties traditionally concern the processes of student discipline, as well as the administration of formal examinations.

prostitution Victorian responses to sex work were driven on the one hand by Christian-inflected moral outrage and on the other by the need to restrict the spread of incurable and debilitating **venereal diseases** such as **syphilis**. The patriarchal nature of both the Church and the medical profession ensured that it was the prostitute – who was in essence engaging in an economic activity – who became both culturally demonised and subjected to statute law, rather than the client who purchased her favours. A more severe stigma was attached to **homosexual** liaisons, where the client was equally as likely to receive a significant punishment, such as **penal servitude** with **hard labour**, as his associate. Brothels and **houses of assignation** catering for both heterosexual and homosexual clients were routinely raided by the police, and prostitutes harassed particularly in the environs of theatres and railway stations. In the late 1860s a series of so-called *Contagious Diseases Acts* were passed in order to suppress prostitution in garrison towns and seaports, these being repealed in 1886. See also: **gay; Labouchère Amendment; lock hospital.**

Protestant A member of any mainstream Christian church, other than the Greek and Russian Orthodox Churches, which does not recognise the spiritual authority of the pope. The Protestant churches – which include the **Anglican, Methodist,** Baptist and Presbyterian communions – characteristically reject the **Roman Catholic** doctrine of transubstantiation within the **Eucharist,** in which the consecrated bread and wine are presumed to become *literally* the body and blood of Christ, as well as the sacraments of confession and the role of saints and the Virgin Mary as intercessors between man and the deity.

THE GREAT SOCIAL EVIL.

Time:—Midnight. A Sketch not a Hundred Miles from the Haymarket.

Bella. "Ah ! Fanny ! How long have you been Gay !"

Figure 26 Prostitutes soliciting in London's theatre-land. John Leech, 'The Great Social Evil', *Punch*, 10 January 1857.

Protestant Alliance, the An **evangelical** and **Protestant** organisation founded in 1845 by Anthony Ashley-Cooper (1801–85), 7th Earl of Shaftesbury, in response to both the rise of the **Oxford Movement** and what was perceived as the increasing influence of the **Roman Catholic** Church. The alliance published a regular newsletter, organised meetings, liaised with sympathetic peers, politicians and clergymen, and erected memorials on the site of historic martyrdoms. A separate Protestant Truth Society was founded by John Kensit (1853–1902) in 1889. See also: **Catholic Truth Society**.

pshaw! An expression of impatience or disgust. See also: **pooh!**

public execution The public hanging of felons, once regarded as a deterrent to those contemplating the commission of similar crimes, was ended by the *Capital Punishment Amendment Act* (31 & 32 Vict. c. 24) of 1868, a measure which also provided for the burial of the executed body within the prison walls.

public houses Premises upon which beer, wines and spirits might be purchased and consumed were regulated under several parliamentary acts from the 1830 *Beerhouse Act* (11 Geo. 4 and 1

Will. 4 c. 64), which liberalised the granting of licensing to publicans, to legislation in 1848 which restricted Sunday opening. The pious and uncompromising rhetoric of organisations such as the **Salvation Army** and **Methodist** Church often demonised the public house as a raucous alternative to sober reflection in church, and castigated the drinker as a selfish individual who neglected family life. Despite this, the congenial **gin palace**, with its warmth and bright illumination, continued to provide a place of pleasure and forgetfulness for the working classes and a taste of the exotic and the dangerous for gentlemen exploring the urban underworld. See also: **Skeleton Army; temperance.**

public schools In British usage, not those schools provided by the State for the education of ordinary citizens but rather the fee-paying and often ancient institutions to which the wealthy and influential sent their male children. The organisational paradigm and curriculum were dominated by practice in the most ancient of the public schools, namely Winchester (founded in 1382), Eton (1440), Rugby (1567) and Harrow (1572), while the work of Thomas Arnold (1795–1842) at Rugby was particularly influential in the shaping of later colleges – such as Marlborough (1843) and Clifton (1862) – on the principle of *mens sana in corpore sano*. The characteristic regime of team sports and Classical learning was also applied to those **grammar schools,** such as the Liverpool Collegiate School (founded 1840), which were originally established as private educational establishments but later administered by the cities whose citizens they served. Equivalent educational opportunities for girls were considerably more limited in the nineteenth century, with Cheltenham Ladies College (founded 1853) establishing a paradigm for academic practice which was to underwrite female admission to British **universities** from 1869.

puerperal fever A fever associated with childbirth, the symptoms of which are a heightened temperature, debility and abdominal pain. Associated with poor hygiene, it frequently proved fatal to the mother who had recently given birth.

pukka A Punjabi word denoting correct, bona fide or authentic. See also: **sahib.**

Punch Subtitled *The London Charivari* – a charivari being a serenade of discordant sounds or a babel of noise – *Punch* was a weekly satirical magazine, first published in 1841, which was distinguished not merely by its humour but also its acute use of cartoons to accentuate the political and social issues of the day.

punkah A swinging fan, usually of cloth or canvas mounted on a frame, worked with a rope by a punkah-wallah. Before the development of electric fans, punkahs were the primary mode of cooling interior spaces in hot climates. The word is derived from Hindi.

Puseyite A follower or supporter of the **Oxford Movement**. The name acknowledges the influence of the theologian and academic Edward Bouverie Pusey (1800–82).

Q

QC A post-nominal designation which indicates that its possessor is a **Queen's Counsel**.

quarter days The four days fixed by ancient custom on which rents fall due, tenancies begin and end, and certain other quarterly charges are traditionally paid. In England and Ireland the quarter days are Lady Day (25 March), Midsummer Day (24 June), Michaelmas (29 September) and Christmas (25 December). The Scottish equivalents are Candlemas (2 February), Whit Sunday (15 May), Lammas (1 August) and Martinmas (11 November).

quarter sessions In England and Ireland, a court which has civil and criminal jurisdiction and which sits quarterly under a **Justice of the Peace**.

Queen Charlotte's Ball An annual ball, first held in 1788 under royal patronage, and a central event within the **London season**. See also: **debutante**.

Queen's Counsel A **barrister** appointed as a legal counsel to the Crown. Queen's Counsels take precedence over other barristers, wear a silk rather than cloth gown in court – their appointment by the Lord Chancellor is popularly known as 'taking silk' – and use the post-nominal QC (or KC, when appointed under a male monarch) to distinguish their status in official correspondence.

Queen's University of Ireland Established by Royal **Charter** on 3 September 1850 as the degree-awarding body for the three Queen's Colleges established in Belfast, Cork and Galway, the Queen's University facilitated university-level education within Ireland for all religious denominations, Trinity College Dublin being predominantly and culturally a **Protestant** institution. The degree-awarding powers of the Queen's University were assumed by the Royal University of Ireland in 1880, this latter body granting degrees to women equivalent to those awarded to men from 1884. See also: **universities; Victoria University.**

Queer Street An imaginary street where individuals in financial distress or likely to be declared bankrupt are figuratively supposed to reside.

queer the pitch To spoil the business of a street vendor, or to damage the impact of stage comedy or acting by distracting the audience.

quinine A bitter-tasting alkaloid, used in the treatment of malaria, and one of the conventional ingredients in commercial tonic water.

R

radical A term which is – somewhat loosely – used to describe a number of areas of British political progressivism. Liberal rather than truly socialist in flavour, radicalism was arguably as much the prerogative of the middle classes as it was of the proletariat – witness, for example, the speakers and the audience gathered at **Peterloo.** Fundamentally, radicalism argued for change – though not always a drastic revision of current conditions of social and financial conditions – and radicals espoused such causes as parliamentary representation and suffrage, the repeal of the **Corn Laws, free trade** more broadly, and the **disestablishment** of the **Anglican** Church. Though influential, radicalism had no central organisation or singular leading figure. See also: **Chartism.**

railway mania A speculative boom in financial investment in Britain's **railway** network in the mid-1840s, which was followed by a crash in the value of railway stocks (instruments of partial ownership) in 1847. The most prominent railway speculator of the day, George Hudson (1800–71) – the so-called Railway King – was subsequently exposed for the irregularity of his financial transactions, was declared bankrupt and fled abroad in order to avoid incarceration in a **debtors' prison.**

railway time The convention by which, from 1840, official timepieces across the United Kingdom were synchronised at London Time rather than being calibrated by the local zenith of the sun. The Great Western **Railway** instituted railway time in order to allow a standardisation of its timetabled services: local clocks, such as those on church towers and civic buildings, soon followed the example, and the convention was progressively adapted across the whole country.

railways Railed tramways, used primarily to convey minerals across relatively short distances between mines and places of processing or distribution precede the nineteenth century. These were initially horse-drawn or pulled by human strength, though a steam locomotive was demonstrated as early as 1825 on the Stockton and Darlington Railway. Passenger haulage under steam power became routine following the opening of the Liverpool and Manchester Railway in 1830, and from that point an unplanned but intercity network of largely regional private companies developed across England, and in Ireland from 1834. By 1870 the railway system outside of Ireland comprised some 21,700 km of track, to which might be added an Irish network of less than 5,000 km. In England, British railway coaches were divided into first, second and third classes, the London **underground** system also providing a separate category of cheap workmen's trains defined by time of travel rather than nature of the accommodation provided.

Rainhill Trials A competition organised by the owners of the Liverpool and Manchester **Railway** in October 1829 during which rival designs for locomotives were compared. The winner was *Rocket*, built by George (1781–1848) and Robert (1803–59) Stephenson.

raj A Hindi word appropriated to signify the direct British rule of India between 1858 and 1947, following the decline of the **East India Company**.

raja From the Hindi, signifying an Indian king or prince or, on occasion, a high-ranking official acting on their behalf. See also: **maharaja**.

Ratcliff Highway. A thoroughfare in the East End of London with a reputation for both crime and **opium** dens.

ratepayer An individual of either sex who was liable to make periodic payments for local administration (most notably the **Poor Law** and certain local or municipal amenities) on account of owning or administering property of a certain value. Liability to pay rates could bring entitlement to vote in parliamentary elections, though the **Reform Acts** specifically excluded women from the national franchise even where they were permitted a vote in municipal governance from 1869.

ratiocination The mental processes through which an accurate conclusion is reached through rational and logical thinking rather than by instinct. The sexist nature of Victorian medicine associated ratiocination with the male brain, and intuition or instinct with the female.

rational dress Though the rational dress movement nominally advocated the design of garments for both sexes based upon practical utility rather than fashion, its interest in women's clothing was perennially topical even after the **Bloomer costume** failed to gain wide acceptance. A Society for Rational Dress was formed in London in 1881, and campaigned against restrictive clothing such as the **corset**, high heels and voluminous skirts.

Rebecca Riots A series of occasionally violent protests against living conditions in rural South Wales between 1839 and 1843. The attacks were particularly focused upon the tollgates which granted paid access to privately maintained roads, though **workhouses** were also damaged by the rioters who, in some cases, were men disguised as women. The name is an allusion to Genesis 24:60.

Rechabites In full, the Independent Order of Rechabites, a **friendly society** with a fraternal structure, founded by Manchester **Methodists** in 1835, membership of which was restricted to those who had signed 'The Pledge' – a formal promise to embrace **temperance** and abstain from the consumption of alcohol. The allusion is to Jeremiah 35:6.

red box A secure and sturdy wooden container, covered with red leather and bearing the royal monogram, which is used by ministers of state to contain and transport official papers.

Reform Acts A colloquial generalisation used to describe legislation to widen the parliamentary franchise enacted in 1832, 1867 and 1884 – a period in which the electoral distinctions between urban boroughs and agricultural counties were progressively reduced while the qualification of voters through personal wealth endured, albeit with modifications. The 1832 *Representation of the People Act* (2 & 3 Will. 4 c. 45) – commonly known as the Great Reform Act – disenfranchised a number of constituencies while creating several new ones and widened the franchise to include small landowners, tenant farmers and shopkeepers, but formally excluded the few women whose property entitled them to vote. The 1867 *Representation of the People Act* (<u>30 & 31 Vict. c. 102</u>) almost doubled the existing franchise in England and Wales by extending the vote to all householders in the boroughs as well as lodgers who paid rent of £10 a year or more, and reduced the property threshold in the counties to enfranchise agricultural landowners and tenants with relatively small amounts of land. Though John Stuart Mill (1806–73) proposed extending the vote to women during the 1867 debate, there was little enthusiasm for female enfranchisement within an exclusively male political system. The 1884 *Representation of the People Act* (**48 & 49 Vict. c. 3**) established a uniform franchise across the United Kingdom by removing the distinction between borough and county voters, and opening up the right to vote to around 58 per cent of the adult male population. It should be noted though that throughout the Victorian period the voting age was set at the age of **majority** – twenty-one years – and that women did not gain the right to vote until 1918, when the male franchise was also separated from a property qualification. The property qualification was, however, retained for female voters with those eligible further required to be over the age of thirty. Some unmarried female ratepayers were granted a vote in local elections under the 1869 *Municipal Franchise Act* (32 & 33 Vict. c. 55), this effective property qualification being (again, selectively) extended to married women under the 1894 *Local Government Act* (56 & 57 Vict. c. 73).

Reform Club, the A London club for gentlemen, founded in 1836 for the benefit of **radicals** and **Whigs** who supported the Great **Reform Act** of 1832. The club became the political headquarters of the **Liberal Party**. Women were first admitted as members in 1981.

Reform League See: **Hyde Park Riots**.

Religious Tract Society Often abbreviated RTS, an **evangelical** publisher of tracts, morally uplifting and often illustrated fiction and periodicals, the latter including *The Boy's Own Paper* and *The Girl's Own Paper*.

repeater A pocket watch with a mechanism which chimed ('repeated') the most recent hour when a lever or spring was touched.

republicanism Though never a coherent movement in nineteenth-century Britain, anti-monarchical sentiment undoubtedly motivated at least some of those attending protests such as **Peterloo** and the **Hyde Park Riots**. The withdrawal of Queen Victoria (1819–1901) from public life during her long period of **mourning** fuelled a certain popularity for the abolition of the hereditary monarchy, though the most powerful advocates came not from the working classes but rather out of the parliamentary system, Charles Bradlaugh (1833–91) and Charles Dilke (1843–1911) being among the most noteworthy proponents of a statutorily achieved British Republic modelled upon the established French civil practice rather than theoretical socialism.

resurrection men A colloquial and ironic term for grave robbers who supplied **surgeons** and medical schools with cadavers for anatomical dissection prior to the 1832 *Anatomy Act* (2 & 3 Will. 4 c. 75). This latter legislation permitted clinicians to make use of bodies left unclaimed by relatives following death in a hospital or **workhouse** as well as the corpses of deceased prisoners.

Ribbonmen An exclusively **Roman Catholic** and largely rural secret society, formed in Ireland in opposition to the **Orangemen** around 1810, which engaged in sectarian violence across the north-eastern province of Ulster well into the mid-century.

Riot Act *The Riot Act* (1 Geo.1 St. 2 c. 5) of 1714 permitted local officials such as **magistrates** or mayors to publically read a proclamation ordering illegally assembled groups of more than twelve individuals to disperse. A subsequent refusal to disperse was deemed an offence, and the use of force to disperse the crowd and to bring any individual involved in the demonstration into official custody was justified. *The Riot Act* was formally read at **Peterloo**. The term was on occasion used colloquially (and sometimes humorously) where a warning had been issued, for example, during a marital dispute.

Risorgimento The collective name for an often fragmented Italian political movement advocating the unification of Italy, many members of which sought exile in Britain. A pervasive but popular myth connected the Risorgimento with earlier Italian secret societies, and with often exaggerated implications of assassination and terrorism associated also with **anarchism**.

ritualism The policy adopted by the **high-church** tendency within the **Anglican** Church which proposed a readoption of certain liturgical ceremonies and church decorations resembling those preceding the **Protestant** Reformation. Ritualist practices included the use of the **Roman Catholic** term 'Mass' to designate the **Eucharist**; the revival of priestly confession; the ritual use of incense, candles, statuary and Latin chants, and the wearing of colourful vestments by the clergy. See also: **Oxford Movement; Puseyite.**

Rochdale Pioneers The Rochdale Equitable Pioneers Society was founded in 1844 by a group of twenty-eight artisans employed in the Lancashire cotton industry, and was instrumental in the founding of a nationwide **co-operative movement**. Pooling financial resources enabled the pioneers to buy basic foodstuffs – flour, oatmeal, sugar and butter – in bulk at a favourable price, and this discount was passed on to the customers who, in turn, became subscribing members of the business, and shared in both the profits and the making of its trading policy.

Roman Catholicism Though nominally the largest global Christian denomination, the Roman Catholic Church has been historically a minority faith in England, Scotland and Wales following the **Protestant** Reformation. Under various acts of legislation – the repeal of which began in 1829 with **Catholic emancipation** – English Roman Catholics were debarred from the franchise, from admission to those **universities** associated with the **Anglican** Church, and from certain professions and public offices. Similar legislation restricted the position of Roman Catholics in Scotland, though it was in Ireland – where a significant Roman Catholic majority was governed by a minority Protestant ascendancy – that doctrinal difference was felt most acutely, and where sectarian adherence frequently became a defining factor in cultural and nationalistic identity.

Romanticism A movement in European art, music, literature and aesthetics in part built upon the supernatural and sublime precedent of the eighteenth-century **Gothic**, but expressing also concern with the environmental and cultural changes consequent upon industrialisation and urban development. Romanticism coloured the artistic representation of working-class life – particularly in rural context – as well as expression of emotion in literary culture, its presence being clearly discernible in mid-century works such as *Wuthering Heights* (1847) by Emily Brontë (1818–48) and, in arguably a more debased form, the pathos of popular **melodrama**.

rookery An urban district, usually regarded as a slum, in which houses have been built in close juxtaposition and are often let by the room as lodgings. In London, the rookeries of Jacob's Island, Seven Dials and St Giles gained a particular notoriety, in part through the writings of **social explorers** and novelists such as Charles Dickens (1812–70) and Charles Kingsley (1819–75).

ropewalk A long and straight passageway, often roofed, in which cordage is formed through the twisting together of shorter and lighter strands of hemp. Prior to the development of steam-powered vessels, strong and durable rope was essential for both the raising and lowering of heavy canvas sails and in the securing of vessels while at anchor or in port. Traditionally a labour-intensive industry, steam-powered mechanisation was introduced progressively to British naval and commercial ropeworks from the 1840s.

Royal University of Ireland See: **Queen's University of Ireland.**

rugby football Based in part upon an ancient and informal tradition of village ball sports and in part upon a **public school** game, the rules and etiquette of rugby were formally codified through the founding of the Rugby Football Union (RFU) in London in 1871. National Unions were formed for Scotland in 1873, Ireland in 1879 and Wales in 1880. An International Rugby Board was formed in 1886. The continued insistence of the RFU that the game be a strictly amateur pursuit prompted a schism in 1895, when twenty-one clubs in northern England withdrew to form the Northern Union, establishing a version of the sport popularly known as rugby league in which the players, who were often industrial shift-workers, could be paid in order to compensate them for lost earnings.

rum An alcoholic spirit, distilled from **sugar** cane and particularly associated with the Royal Navy. British imperial interests in the West Indies led to the adoption of rum over other spirits, and a formal 70 ml rum ration (known as a 'tot') was issued daily to most sailors (the exceptions being those under the **age of majority**, those committed to **temperance**, and senior officers whose access to spirits, including gin, was less restricted). Rum mixed with water was known as grog. The order to 'splice the mainbrace' signifies the award of an additional tot to each member of the crew in recognition of good service.

runcible spoon A nonsense term invented by Edward Lear (1812–88) in 1870 which, nonetheless, was subsequently applied to a peculiarly angled piece of cutlery which combined the shape of a conventional spoon with the prongs of a fork.

Russian bath See: **Turkish bath.**

S

sahib A respectful title, the equivalent of 'sir', which would be customarily used by an Indian imperial subject when addressing an Englishman or other European. The term '**pukka** sahib' denotes an individual considered by the speaker to be socially respectable – a 'true gentleman'.

sal volatile An aromatic solution of ammonium carbonate, commonly used as a restorative to relieve a fit of fainting. See also: **smelling salts.**

Salvation Army An **evangelical** organisation founded in 1865 as the Christian Mission and reorganised upon quasi-military lines from 1878. The uniformed organisation preached a practical Christianity of 'soup, soap and salvation' to the urban working classes, with a specific emphasis upon **temperance.** See also: **Skeleton Army.**

Sam Browne A military belt which passes around the wearer's waist and is further supported by a strap which extends diagonally over the body from the left front-side of the belt over the right shoulder and back to left rear-side of the belt. It was invented by General Sir Sam Browne **VC** (1824–1901), following the **Indian Mutiny.**

Sapphism A euphemism derived from the name of the Classical poet Sappho (c.610–c.570 BCE), for female same-sex desire. See also: **homosexuality.**

savings banks Originated in Scotland in 1810 by the **Protestant** clergyman Henry Duncan (1774–1846), an initially local system which permitted those on a low income to save money through an interest-bearing bank account. The movement spread across Britain within five years, though coverage was not uniform, prompting William Ewart Gladstone (1809–98) to propose a government-backed scheme organised around the national Post Office system in 1861.

Savoy Opera A series of comic – and often highly topical – **operas** associated with the librettist William Schwenck Gilbert (1836–1911) and the composer Arthur Sullivan (1842–1900), performed between 1871 and 1901. The name references the Savoy Theatre in London, which was built by the impresario Richard D'Oyly Carte (1844–1901) in 1881. Among the best known are *HMS Pinafore* (1878), *Patience* (1881) and *The Mikado* (1885). See also: **greenery-yallary.**

séance Popularly, a meeting at which the claims of **spiritualism** are purportedly demonstrated, though the term was also on occasion applied to investigative gatherings exhibiting **mesmerism.**

Season See: **London season.**

secularism A broad movement which variously rejected the existence of a presiding deity and eschewed the presence of a spiritual dimension to human existence, and which also proposed the removal of ecclesiastical influence in politics and civil administration. A National Secular Society was founded in 1866 by the atheist Charles Bradlaugh (1833–91), who became a **Liberal Party** MP in 1880. Bradlaugh's refusal to swear a religious oath in order to take his seat in the **House of Commons** prompted a number of by-elections in which he was successively returned, his attempts to cast his vote within Parliament in this period being technically illegal. The *Oaths Act* of 1888 (51 & 52 Vict. c. 46) permitted an individual to make a solemn affirmation in place of an oath declared before God.

self-help A pervasive doctrine of familial thrift, personal independence and moralised hard work popularised through the book *Self-Help; with Illustrations of Character and Conduct*, published in 1859 by Samuel Smiles (1812–1904). In this and other works, Smiles, a Scot with experience in **Chartism** and parliamentary reform, advanced the personal achievements of self-made industrialists and entrepreneurs as a model for the betterment of artisans, emphasising not merely their perseverance but also the advantages of **temperance** and moderation, honesty and integrity, industriousness and education.

sensation fiction A genre of Victorian popular fiction, influenced by both the **Gothic novel** and **melodrama**, and characterised by narratives of crime, mystery and social scandal. Sensation fiction was well adapted to both expose and explore the difficulties which women faced under the laws and customs which underwrote marriage and inheritance in particular, and in consequence proved a durably popular medium for female writers and readers. The most prominent writers in the genre included Mary Elizabeth Braddon (1835–1915), Wilkie Collins (1824–89) and Ellen Wood (1814–87).

servants See: **butler; boots; footman; groom; housekeeper; maid of all work; valet.**

sett In urban usage, an artificially squared stone block, often of granite, which forms part of a paved road surface; in rural usage, a badger's burrow. See also: **cobblestones.**

sexton An individual, usually male but sometimes female, employed by a church as a general caretaker. A sexton's duties would typically include digging graves and tolling the church bell for **funerals** as well as sweeping the building.

shagreen A type of rough untanned leather, made from shark or seal skin or horsehide.

shilling A unit of pre-decimal **currency** representing twelve pennies.

shooting See: **game; pheasant shooting.**

shooting box A small country house occupied during the **shooting** season, and customarily used for entertaining as well as accommodation.

shooting stick A strong walking stick with a handle that opens up to form a seat.

shorthand Though individual techniques that enabled rapid notetaking were employed across the century in commercial practice, the first widely adopted shorthand system – the Stenographic Sound Hand – was developed in 1837 by Isaac Pitman (1813–97) and used simple abbreviations based upon the sounds of the words dictated.

shrapnel shell A hollow projectile containing metallic shot and an explosive charge, formally adopted as a weapon by the British Army in 1803. This exploding projectile was known as spherical case shot until 1853.

side-saddle A saddle upon which the rider sits with both legs positioned on the same side, the horse being controlled in part through the use of a long riding whip. Side-saddles were conventionally regarded as appropriate for female riders engaged in **hunting** and other equestrian activities because they accommodated the rider's long skirts or riding habits – breeches being regarded as uniquely male attire – and also because riding astride was considered medically inadvisable, if not immodest, for horsewomen.

Skeleton Army An informally constituted and largely working-class counterpart to the **Salvation Army,** organised primarily on ad hoc and local lines and engaged in sometimes violent (and, on occasion, fatal) acts of opposition to the public marches and **temperance** crusades of the **evangelical** organisation. Skeleton violence peaked in the 1880s and declined in the final decade of the century.

slavery As a British imperial practice, slavery can be dated to the sixteenth century, the importance of enslaved labour increasing as the domestic taste for imported commodities such as sugar, **rum**

and tobacco developed in the eighteenth and nineteenth centuries. As well as conveying slaves from Africa to British colonies such as Jamaica, British vessels and trading houses were also implicated in supporting the slave economy of the United States – a major source of cotton for the mills of the English north. Organised agitation against British involvement in the global slave trade began in the late eighteenth century, with Quaker and mainstream Christian groups often shaping the debate. In 1807 the *Slave Trade Act* (47 Geo. 3 Sess. 1 c. 36) rendered 'the Purchase, Sale, Barter or Transfer of Slaves' illegal but did not liberate those already enslaved. Many slave traders continued to flout the law even though the Royal Navy established a West African Squadron in 1808 specifically to intercept slaving vessels and release their captives. In 1833 the *Slavery Abolition Act* (3 & 4 Will. 4 c. 73) effectively freed some 800,000 slaves in British territories in the Caribbean, South Africa and Canada, but not those enslaved by the **East India Company**, or located in Ceylon (now Sri Lanka) and St Helena. British citizens who had invested in colonial slaves were generously compensated under the *Slave Compensation Act* (<u>1 & 2 Vict. c. 3</u>) of 1837. The ostensibly liberated slaves, however, were not returned to their homelands and were forced to negotiate often highly unfavourable terms of employment – frequently as **indentured labour** – with their former masters. British cotton mills, however, were still dependent upon raw materials produced by enslaved labour in the United States following the effective abolition of slavery across the whole of the British Empire in 1843.

small beer A beer of low alcoholic strength, often brewed within larger households, and used as an everyday beverage on account of it being less contaminated by organic infection than unboiled and unfiltered water. See also: **cholera**.

smelling salts A preparation of carbonate of ammonia, commonly used as a restorative in cases of fainting or light-headedness. See also: **sal volatile**.

smoking See: **briar**; **cheroot**; **cigarette**; **meerschaum**; **Trichinopoly cigar**.

snooker A development of the earlier game of **billiards**, devised by British Army officers stationed in Jubbulpore, India, in 1875. The game was introduced to Britain in 1885.

snuff Powdered (and sometimes flavoured) tobacco inhaled through the nostrils as a stimulant.

social exploration A movement inspired in part by **evangelical** zeal, but motivated also by journalists seeking to satisfy the curiosity of the middle classes, which reported upon the lives and morals of the – predominantly urban – working classes from mid-century. The reportage of social exploration customarily drew upon spectacle, emphasising colourful characters and morals unfamiliar to its target readership, and often freighted this with moral messages regarding **temperance** and the perceived improvidence or laziness of the working and criminal classes. The City of London proved an enduring focus, and the influence of fictionalists such as Charles Dickens (1812–70) and Arthur Morrison (1863–1945) must be understood as contributing to the style of the genre. Representative works in the tradition include *London Labour and the London Poor* (1851) by Henry Mayhew (1812–87), *The Bitter Cry of Outcast London* (1883) by Andrew Mearns (1837–1925) and *In Darkest England, and the Way Out* (1890) by William Booth (1829–1912), the founder of the **Salvation Army**. The title of this last volume patronisingly associated the domestic poor with colonial subjects through its allusion to *In Darkest Africa* (1890) by the explorer Henry Morton Stanley (1841–1904).

Society for Psychical Research Founded in 1882, a learned organisation formed by scientists, philosophers and other prominent academics to systematically investigate supposedly occult phenomena including clairvoyance, hauntings, **mesmerism, spiritualism** and **theosophy**.

Society for the Suppression of Vice Instituted in 1802, an organisation which actively campaigned against the spread of perceived immorality and vice, particularly where these were made available to the public through publications, illustrations and theatrical performance. The agents of the society engaged in the effective entrapment of **pornographers** through the purchase of publications, and pursued the publishers as well as vendors of such centres as **Holywell Street** through the courts in order to destroy their stock and imprison or substantially fine the proprietors. The society was absorbed into the similarly motivated **National Vigilance Association** in 1885.

Soho A district of the West End of London long associated with the sex industry but also, in the nineteenth century, with immigrant populations and political dissidence. See also: **cholera**.

Figure 27 A sola topee, worn by an explicitly English imperialist, who is proffering his word (in the form of a treaty) to a derogatively stereotyped African leader. Illustration from Mrs E. A. Ames, *ABC for Baby Patriots* (1899).

sola topee A lightweight domed helmet made of dried pith, covered with **khaki** cloth, worn as protection against the tropical sun.

Somerville College Proposed as a non-denominational 'Ladies Hall' within the **University** of Oxford in 1878, Somerville Hall opened in 1879, though its students were permitted neither to attend lectures nor to take degrees. Lectures in some – but not all – academic subjects were opened to women across the 1880s, and women were permitted to sit examinations in 1884. Somerville Hall formally became a college in 1894, though female graduates were not actually awarded degrees by the university until 1920. See also: **clubs**.

Spa Fields Riot A public disturbance on 2 December 1816, starting at Spa Fields in Islington, London, when a number of **Spencean Philanthropists** organised an unsuccessful attack on the Tower of London. Four of the leaders were subsequently charged with high treason, though the case failed when their defence counsel argued that they had been entrapped by a government agent provocateur.

spat An ankle-length gaiter which covers the upper part of the shoe and protects it from damage by moisture or dirt.

Special Branch In full, the Special (Irish) Branch, a unit of the Metropolitan **Police**, formed in 1883 specifically to combat the threat posed by Irish republican organisations. The jurisdiction of the unit was later expanded to include the investigation (and arrest) of individuals involved in **anarchism**, bolshevism and the campaigns of the **suffragette** movement. See also: **Fenian**.

Spencean Philanthropists See: **Cato Street Conspiracy**.

spermaceti A waxy substance found in the head of the sperm whale and used in the manufacture of candles.

spermatic economy A term coined by G. J. Barker Benfield in 1972 to describe the popular Victorian association between blood and semen. Deriving from an earlier – and inaccurate – understanding of reproductive biology, this enduring assumption viewed semen as an occluded product of blood, and suggested that any discharge of seminal fluid would provoke a corresponding bloodlessness that would manifest itself in customary symptoms including pale and clammy skin and a general lassitude or weakness. See also: **onanism**.

spherical case shot See: **shrapnel shell**.

spirit photography The developing technology of Victorian **photography** permitted not merely the accurate capture of monochrome images but also their manipulation. From the 1860s the duplicitous double-exposure of photographic plates facilitated the production of images which purportedly juxtaposed dead individuals alongside the living subject, particularly those sitters involved in **spiritualism**.

spiritualism A religious movement, though not necessarily one organised as a discrete denomination, whose core beliefs embrace the survival of individual identity following death and an assumption that the dead are both willing and able to communicate with the living. Modern spiritualism came to Britain from the United States at mid-century and drew upon the conventions of intangible sources of power present in the orthodox sciences such as electricity and magnetism as well as in pseudosciences such as **mesmerism**. In the darkened **séance** room, the dead reputedly manifested themselves through rapping noises and table-turning, in **spirit photography** and by writing messages via instruments such as the **planchette**. Though investigations by individuals as well as the **Society for Psychical Research** discredited many mediums, the movement nonetheless survived as an adjunct to mainstream Christianity and in the institution of the Spiritualist National Union, founded in 1901.

Spithead A channel adjoining Portsmouth, one of the most important home ports for the Royal Navy, used as a mustering point and anchorage for fighting vessels.

spooney The condition of being foolish or sentimental, particularly where romantic love is concerned.

spring gun A small firearm, usually activated by a trip wire, commonly set to deter (or to actually wound) trespassers or poachers, particularly on estates where **game** is raised.

Spring-Heeled Jack A figure in both urban mythology and popular literature, supposedly capable of leaping to the height of a building, whose activities were first reported in London in 1838 with later sightings regularly reported across England as late as 1904.

spud A narrow-bladed digging implement utilised for agricultural or domestic weeding. In Kent, the term refers to a three-pronged tool used for similar purposes.

squire A colloquial term often applied (sometimes in the form of a prefix) to a country gentleman.

St James's An exclusive residential and commercial district in the West End of London. The area includes the royal residences of Buckingham and St James's Palaces, extensive parks, the National Gallery (opened in 1824), the National Portrait Gallery (founded 1856) and the fashionable tailoring establishments of **Jermyn Street**.

stagecoach A horse-drawn vehicle which runs to a schedule between two destinations, making intermediate stops to change horses and pick up passengers and mail. Stagecoach services, which were often evocatively named, customarily carried passengers at a premium fare inside the carriage, and a number of outside passengers, who enjoyed no protection from inclement weather, to the front and rear of the conveyance's roof. Though relatively reliable in terms of punctuality, stagecoach services declined from the 1830s as a consequence of the development of the **railways**.

stamp duty A tax levied initially upon paper and print media – such as newspapers, pamphlets, advertisements and playing cards – stamp duty was extended at various times to cover a range of physical products, such as patent medicines, as well as the formal licences to practise which were issued to solicitors and **pawnbrokers** and the legal paperwork which formalised the employment of **apprentices**. The abolition of the stamp duty levied upon newsprint from 15 June 1855 by way of the *Newspapers Act* (18 & 19 Vict. c. 27), and the removal in 1860 of a separate duty levied upon paper, prompted many existing periodicals to reduce their prices, as well as facilitating the launch of cheap newspapers marketed to an increasingly literate working class. The term 'stamp duty' survives in modern British usage in association with land taxation.

stays A female undergarment braced with whalebone or steel, used to compress the waistline and provide shape and support to the torso. See also: **corset**.

steamships Experiments in steam-powered navigation began independently in France, Britain and the United States in the closing quarter of the eighteenth century, with a successful passenger service operating from Glasgow as early as 1812. The first transatlantic navigation was achieved seven years later, though regular services were initiated only in 1838 via the SS *Great Western*, a paddle-steamer designed by Isambard Kingdom Brunel (1806–59), supplemented by the iron-hulled SS *Great Britain* in 1843. Transatlantic mail services were contracted to the Cunard Line in 1840. Paddle-steamers were superseded by propeller- (or 'screw-') driven vessels from the later 1860s, this technology providing both greater speed and stability in rough seas.

stearine A plant-based fatty acid used in the manufacture of candles in preference to **tallow** or beeswax. Unlike tallow, stearine is odourless when the candlewick is alight.

steeplechase Also known as National Hunt racing, a horse race in which the participants are required to jump various barriers which may include hurdles, ditches and water jumps. Flat racing, the alternative form of competitive equestrianism, does not feature jumps. See also: **Grand National, the**.

stereoscope A **photographic** device employing two viewing lenses and a pair of images taken at slightly different angles in order to produce a three-dimensional image.

stillroom A room in a private house or hotel in which cakes and preserves are kept and where tea or coffee is prepared by a **servant** known as a stillroom maid.

stone-breaking The breaking-up of large stones into smaller fragments, often imposed as menial employment for men in the **workhouse** system or as punitive **hard labour** for convicted prisoners.

Strand Magazine An illustrated monthly magazine, founded in 1891, with a particular reputation for fiction and a long association with Sherlock Holmes, a character created in 1887 by Arthur Conan Doyle (1859–1930).

street **Arab** A homeless (and, by definition, peripatetic) child or young person, particularly one who makes a living through petty crime or by providing menial services, such as bootblacking or message-carrying, for ready cash.

strychnine A colourless alkaloid, bitter to the taste, which was occasionally deployed as a poison – most notoriously in the criminal career of Thomas Neill Cream (1850–92).

subaltern In military usage, a junior officer below the rank of captain.

Suez Canal An artificial waterway connecting the Red Sea with the Mediterranean, opened in 1869 and of strategic importance to British imperial and trading interests in the Indian Ocean and Far East.

Suffragette Though the name is often popularly associated with the twentieth-century campaigns of the Women's Social and Political Union, founded in 1903 by Emmeline Pankhurst (1858–1928), its origins lie in the numerous constituent bodies which formed the National Union of Women's Suffrage Societies in 1897. This latter body claimed 1867 as the year in which the first suffrage society was established, and published pamphlets, organised meetings and sought support from Members of Parliament.

sugar The development of efficient refining technology in the form of 'Howard's Vacuum Pan' in 1813 initiated a progressive reduction in the cost of the cane sugar which British distributors sourced from Caribbean islands whose early economies were premised upon **slavery**. Caribbean sugar was also the raw material of **rum,** and an essential ingredient in preserving fruit through jam-making at a time when mechanical refrigeration had not been developed: it was never simply a sweetener.

sugar-nippers A domestic tool for breaking down large pieces of **sugar** into smaller fragments. Prior to the development of the technology which facilitated the manufacture of granulated sugar, the sweetening commodity was transported in so-called sugar loaves – large, hard blocks of various shapes and sizes. In domestic situations, loaf sugar was first 'nipped' into smaller pieces and then finally ground in a pestle and mortar. Sugar tongs were used to handle pieces of lump sugar which were sufficiently small as to be used to sweeten individual cups of tea or coffee.

suicide In Britain, prior to 1961, any attempt to end one's own life was by definition a criminal act – essentially, self-murder – and an unsuccessful suicide was liable to prosecution. See also: **felo de se.**

surgeon A medical professional who specialised in specifically interventive treatment, such as amputations and invasive surgery. See also: **apothecary; physician.**

sweated labour Workers employed at low rates, often undertaking **piecework** for long hours and in the unsanitary workplace conditions of the so-called sweatshops. The sweated industries, which included commercial activities as diverse as the manufacture of clothing or the assembly of matchboxes, also frequently relied upon homeworkers employed by an intermediary who sold the products on at a profit to a finisher or a retailer. Homeworkers operated essentially outside of the employment legislation enacted between 1802 and 1895, and children who could not legally be employed in factories were frequently involved in unregulated domestic sweating.

sweatshop See: **sweated labour.**

Swedenborgian A follower of Emmanuel Swedenborg (1688–1772), a mystical Christian whose doctrines stressed the presence of a spiritual world which coexisted with the known material environment. The Irish **Gothic** writer J. Sheridan Le Fanu (1814–73) was one of several novelists influenced by the teaching of Swedenborg's so-called 'New Church'.

swell A stylish or handsomely dressed individual whose demeanour reflects, for example, the manner of a gentleman about town. Swells, variously villainous or ridiculous, were part of the conventional casting of both **music hall** and theatrical **melodrama.**

Swing Riots A period of unrest between 1830 and 1831 in southern and eastern England during which agricultural workers – supposedly inspired by the fictitious 'Captain Swing' – threatened violence to farmers who introduced threshing machinery, and set fire to buildings and hayricks in response to reductions in their wages. The political response to the disturbances was decisive, with apprehended rioters receiving sentences of imprisonment, **transportation** or **public execution.**

sword stick A blade concealed within a walking cane, which might be carried in public by a gentleman without arousing any suspicion of him being armed.

syphilis A sexually transmitted infection whose presence is commonly signified by genital ulcers, swollen glands in the neck, white sores within the mouth, and skin rashes. Treatment during the nineteenth century was palliative and served only to mask symptoms rather than eradicate their underlying cause. **Mercury**, in particular, was administered both under prescription and in spurious **patent medicines**, the application of this chemical no doubt exacerbating, rather than relieving, the imperilled health of the patient. See also: **venereal disease**.

T

Table of Kindred and Affinity See: *Book of Common Prayer.*

Taff Vale Case A legal judgment following a court case conducted across 1900–1, which determined that **trades unions** could be held liable for the financial losses suffered by employers as a consequence of strike action and picketing. Trades union immunity was restored through legislation enacted in 1906.

tallow A fatty substance, the by-product of the domestic or commercial slaughter of cattle and sheep, used in the manufacture of industrial lubricants and also for the manufacture of cheap candles. Tallow candles, and the cheaper rushlights which are similarly coated in the fat, produce a pervasive organic odour when burned, and a light whose quality may be variable on account of impurities in the substance.

Tamworth Manifesto A political statement delivered by the **Tory** politician Sir Robert Peel (1788–1850) in 1834, which advanced a new policy of cautious reform. Peel's manifesto visibly established his leadership of the **Conservative** Party, and formally ended its essentially unwritten policy of resisting change in national political culture.

Tartanware See: **Mauchline ware**.

Tattersall's The principal betting room at a racecourse and, in consequence, an important meeting place for gamblers, bookmakers and moneylenders. The name is derived from a horse market established by Richard Tattersall (1724–95) in 1766. The venue also lends its name to a fabric for clothes which resembles the pattern of the checked horse blankets used at the market.

tea The ritualised brewing and consumption of tea might be considered as being as central to a pervasive national identity as they were to the regulating of both the working and the social day. Cheap (and, on occasions, **adulterated**) tea, usually taken with milk and

sugar (the latter for energy as much as taste) became a staple of the working-class diet following the development of Indian – as opposed to Chinese – sources of supply from the 1840s. For all social classes, tea proved a safer beverage than water, the process of boiling eradicating the bacilli that transmitted **cholera** and other potentially fatal disorders.

teetotalism A colloquial term for the practice of **temperance**, allegedly derived from an individual's stammered affirmation of his own '(tee)total abstinence' from alcohol, reported in northern England in the early 1830s.

telegraphy A mode of communication whereby messages could be sent along a wire via electrical pulses. A system which used an electrically deflected needle to indicate the component letters of a message was patented in Britain as early as 1837, two years following the development of Morse code in the United States. The Electric Telegraph Company was formed in Britain in 1845 and became part of the Post Office in 1870. Telegraph wires were frequently suspended from poles along the course of existing **railway** lines, with many telegraph offices being located at major stations. See also: **telephone**.

telephone A practical telephone was first exhibited in Britain in 1876, though the invention was doubtlessly popularised when telephony was demonstrated by Alexander Graham Bell (1847–1922) in the presence of Queen Victoria (1819–1901) on the Isle of Wight in 1878 – the royal household subsequently purchasing the equipment on which the monarch had communicated with London. Developed initially through private enterprise and dominated by the National Telephone Company from 1889, the various telephone networks were progressively taken over by the Post Office under legislation proposed in 1892. See also: **telegraphy**.

temperance A broad movement which campaigned against the recreational consumption of alcohol, and actively promoted 'teetotalism' – the total abstention from alcohol. Temperance campaigns were primarily aimed at the working classes, reflecting a middle-class and often **evangelical** distaste for proletarian entertainments and a desire to reform the perceived indolence and ungodliness of the poor. Organisations such as the **Band of Hope** (established 1847) attempted to frustrate a taste for alcohol in children, with established adult drinkers being addressed by dedicated bodies such as the **Rechabites** and **Salvation Army**,

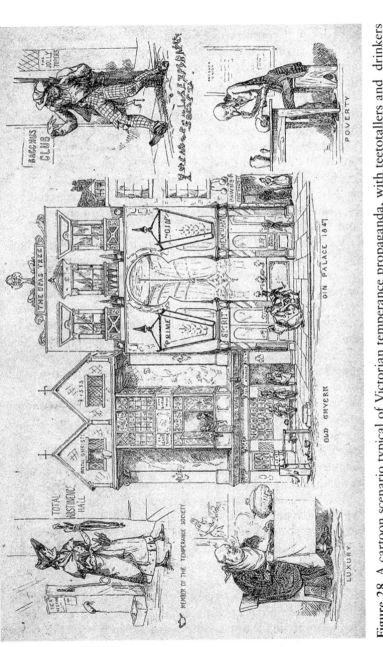

Figure 28 A cartoon scenario typical of Victorian temperance propaganda, with teetotallers and drinkers placed in diametric opposition. Luke Limner (pseud), *The Upas Tree* (1847).

as well as by the **Methodist** churches, which maintained a network of 'Central Halls'. The **Liberal Party** was on occasion associated with the temperance cause through its attempts to impose restrictions upon the consumption of alcohol, particularly in the working-class environment of the urban public house: the 1872 *Licensing Act* (35 & 36 Vict. c. 94), which limited opening hours, criminalised public inebriation, regulated the content of beer and allowed local authorities to restrict or even ban the sale of alcohol, prompted the closure of many beer houses and provoked riots. A National Temperance Federation was founded in 1884, with support from within the Liberal Party.

Temple Bar 'A London magazine for town and country readers', published monthly at the price of one **shilling** between 1860 and 1906.

theatre Victorian theatre was initially shaped by earlier polices which had significantly restricted the number of venues within the City of London and placed restrictions upon the genres which might be performed in metropolitan and provincial playhouses. These restrictions, which applied in particular to the staging of 'serious' drama including the plays of Shakespeare, were repealed by the 1843 *Theatres Act* (6 & 7 Vict. c. 68), though by this time their influence had already stimulated the development of **melodrama** and **music hall** as forms of entertainment attractive to all social classes. The 1843 act imposed licensing restrictions upon plays produced in London and the university cities of Oxford and Cambridge, though its influence upon what might be performed in the provinces was limited.

theosophy A system of occult and mystical beliefs codified by the founders of the Theosophical Society from 1875. Theosophy is monistic, expressing the belief that reality is essentially composed of one spiritual substance under an impersonal deity, with human beings embodying aspects of the divine in material form. The society's first president, Helena Petrovna Blavatsky (1831–91), was investigated by the **Society for Psychical Research** in 1884, an allegation of fraud being levelled against her a year later.

thimblerig Ostensibly a form of gambling where players bet upon the supposed location of a pea placed beneath one of three thimbles, this form of simple amusement was frequently regarded as an exemplar of trickery played upon the naive or unwary.

Thirty-Nine Articles A statement regarding the **Protestant** faith professed by the **Anglican** Church, and a definition of its formal relationship to the **Roman Catholic** Church, which is customarily appended to the *Book of Common Prayer*.

three-volume novel See: triple-decker.

thuggee The practice of robbery and murder, usually by strangulation, practised by devotees of the goddess Kali in India, popularly known as Thugs.

ticket-of-leave A formal licence which entitles an individual to be at large before the end of a custodial sentence. Tickets-of-leave were issued to both domestic prisoners and to those sentenced to **transportation** under the condition that conviction for any further offence would return the individual to custody.

tiffin A term denoting a light midday meal that was particularly associated with imperial culture in India, sometimes applied to the equivalent luncheon in Britain.

tobacco In middle-class culture, smoking embodied a ritual function not dissimilar to **tea** drinking: the lighting of a cigar, or else a **briar**, **calabash** or **meerschaum** pipe, was a gentlemanly prerogative, whether taken with **port** after a meal and away from female company, or else pursued in the equally gendered seclusion of a club or similar environment. The consumption of tobacco by middle-class ladies was for the most part deemed scandalous or exceptional, cigarettes being popularly associated with the iconoclastic behaviour of the **New Woman** later in the century. Working-class women were somewhat freer to join their menfolk in enjoying tobacco: though the pipe was utilised by both sexes, cigarettes came to dominate the market from 1883 when the introduction of new machinery facilitated mass production. Numerous campaigns against smoking were conducted across the century, drawing on both medical and evangelical arguments in a manner reminiscent of the contemporary **temperance** movement, and characteristically targeting the young and the proletariat. A British Anti-Tobacco Society, which published a journal, was extant from mid-century, though substantial legislation against smoking was not achieved until the 1908 *Children Act* (8 Edw. 7 c. 67).

Tolpuddle Martyrs A group of six Dorset **trades union** members who were convicted in 1834 of swearing a secret oath as part of their membership of the **Friendly Society** of Agricultural Labourers. Following domestic incarceration upon **prison hulks**, the six were **transported** to Australia. Public agitation for their release saw the six return piecemeal to Britain between 1837 and 1839, where five of the original Martyrs joined the **Chartist** movement before finally emigrating to Canada.

Tommy Atkins Sometimes abbreviated to 'Tommy', a popular personification of the British soldier. The name was reputedly used as an example to aid the completion of military documents, and gained enduring currency through the 1890 poem 'The Queen's Uniform', more commonly known as 'Tommy' by Rudyard Kipling (1865–1936). See also: **Jack Tar**.

tontine A financial scheme in which subscribers invest collectively in order to fund a personal annuity. On the death of a subscriber, the value of their investment is absorbed by those who remain, their annuity increasing in consequence. The term is sometimes associated with the annual payments distributed to members of **friendly societies**.

tooth powder A dentifrice or dry substance used to clean and polish the teeth.

top boots Riding boots which extend to just below the knee and feature a cuff or panel in a contrasting colour such as white, buff or brown at the top. Top boots are associated with horse racing and with **hunting** particularly, though they were sometimes worn in town as a fashionable accessory. See also: **butcher boots**.

Tory A traditional term which may denote, variously, the membership or policy of the British **Conservative Party**.

town and gown A term for the opposing factions which prototypically may be found in the social and political life of a **university** city, 'town' denoting the indigenous population and their political representatives, 'gown' the members of the university, most frequently the student population but also on occasion the officers and financial interests of the institution.

Toynbee Hall The first **university settlement**, established in the East End of London in 1884 and offering extramural **university** lectures led by faculty and students from Oxford and Cambridge, as well as informal courses and recreational clubs in addition to facilities such as free legal advice.

Tractarianism See: **Oxford Movement**.

Trades Union Congress The central federation of English and Welsh **trades unions**, which first met at the **Mechanics' Institute** in

Manchester in 1868. The congress was formed in the first instance by representatives of the skilled trades, with unskilled unions affiliating after 1889, and in its early years tended to impose campaigning pressure upon Parliament in order to achieve legislation favourable to its membership rather than advocating direct or disruptive action in the form of strikes.

trades unions Though organisations analogous to trades unions can be dated in Britain to the seventeenth century, any attempt at collective action by the working classes was easily contemplated as potentially seditious in a century that witnessed both the **Swing Riots** and the destruction of technology by the **Luddites**. The *Combination Acts* of 1824 (5 Geo. 4 c. 95) and 1825 (6 Geo 4 c. 129) legalised individual affiliation to trades unions while still restricting collective bargaining and the right to picket and strike. The internal structuring of some trades unions as oath-bound societies, however, rendered membership technically illegal under the 1797 *Unlawful Oaths Act* (37 Geo. 3 c. 123), the statute under which the **Tolpuddle Martyrs** were sentenced. Despite legal restriction, trades union membership increased as the century progressed, to reach around a million across the country by 1874. The 1871 *Trade Union Act* (**34 & 35 Vict. c. 31**) established the legal status of trades unions, though the legality of strike action and picketing remained questionable until the **Taff Vale Case**, which led to further legislation in 1906. Though initially excluded by the gendered nature of skilled employment, women were to become increasingly involved in the trades union movement from the 1880s, a period in which unskilled labour was becoming increasingly unionised. See also: **Trades Union Congress**.

transportation Initiated in 1787 and abolished in 1865, a policy in which convicted felons of both sexes might be shipped from Britain to convict colonies in Australia, where they were put to work as effective **slave** labour. There was no provision for the return of convicts following the completion of a sentence, and so many of those transported became involuntary settlers and, on occasion, employers of subsequent convicts. See also: **capital punishment; Luddites; Swing Riots; Tolpuddle Martyrs**.

traps A collective term for baggage or other personal effects under transport.

treadmill A mechanical device, utilised in the administration of **hard labour** as part of **penal servitude**, on which a prisoner was compelled to maintain a constant walking pace in order not to be injured by the rotating steps of the treadmill. Some treadmills were connected to functional machinery for the grinding of flour or other commodities, though others were installed merely as punitive instruments.

Trichinopoly cigar Also known colloquially as a 'Tritchie' or 'Trichie', a relatively cheap cigar or **cheroot**, originally manufactured in Triruchirappalli (sometimes abbreviated to Trichy) in Tamil Nadu, India, and exported to the United Kingdom.

triple-decker A three-volume version of a novel, produced as such to suit the commercial requirements of the **circulating libraries**. A one-volume novel would require a reader to maintain only a single subscription: dividing a longer book into three would effectively force the reader to subscribe to three reader's tickets in order to read the whole work continuously.

truck system The payment of wages in a form other than **currency**. Typically, payment would be made in tokens which might be redeemed only at a store owned by the employer, where goods were often sold at a rate higher than that of a shop freely competing with other businesses. Legislation to restrict the system – the so-called *Truck Acts* – was enacted in 1831 (1 & 2 Will. 4 c. 37), 1887 (50 & 51 Vict. c. 46) and 1896 (59 & 60 Vict. c. 44).

tuberculosis Also known as **phthisis** and **consumption**, an often fatal, and almost invariably debilitating, condition commonly spread by bacterial droplets on the breath. Sufferers were characteristically portrayed in fiction as pallid and languid, their breathing laboured and their sputum flecked with blood. Other common symptoms included a persistent cough which might develop to a point at which fragmented lung tissue was expelled; extremes of temperature, including fevers and free perspiration; and progressive weight loss. Tubercular women, in particular, were sometimes pathologised as sexually rapacious and a moral, as well as physical, danger to their male associates.

Turkish bath A social institution rather than a mere act of cleansing, the heating, induced sweating, cooling and massage associated with the Turkish bath provided an opportunity for homosocial (and, on occasion, **homosexual**) encounters within facilities rigidly divided by gender. Strictly speaking, Turkish baths utilise hot dry air, where Russian baths deploy steam or vapour.

turnpike road A private road, usually authorised by an act of Parliament, where a charge for use is levied upon travellers at tollgates or tollhouses. The turnpike system fell into decline as a consequence of the increased conveyance of goods via the canal and **railway** networks, and had all but disappeared by the close of the century, the few survivals usually being privately owned bridges and short roads across enclosed land.

tussy mussy A small bouquet of flowers and herbs carried in a metallic or ceramic holder, the contents of which were often assembled in accordance with **floriography**.

typhoid fever Any acute infectious disease, such as enteric fever, the symptoms of which – such as headache, a transient rose-coloured rash and abdominal discomfort – resemble those of **typhus**.

typhus An **epidemic** disease, transmitted by body lice in conditions of poor hygiene, the symptoms of which include fever, a progressive red skin rash, and a state of debilitation which can conclude in delirium or stupor. See also: **typhoid fever**.

U

uitlanders An Afrikaans word meaning 'foreigner' or 'outsider', used to describe British immigrants living in the Transvaal and to derogatively distinguish them from **Boer** citizens.

ulster A long, loose overcoat, often featuring a belt, first sold in Belfast in 1867. The name is derived from the name of the northernmost of the four historical provinces of Ireland, Connacht (known officially as Connaught while under British governance), Leinster, Munster and Ulster. Following the formal Partition of Ireland (13 Geo. 5 Sess. 2 c. 2) in 1922, six of the historical nine counties of Ulster – Fermanagh, Armagh, Tyrone, Londonderry, Antrim and Down – remained within the United Kingdom; Cavan, Monaghan and Donegal became part of the twenty-six-county Irish Free State. See also: **Home Rule.**

Ulster custom A tenant right, associated with the province of Ulster in particular, under which an outgoing tenant may receive compensation from the tenant who succeeds him or her for improvements made to the land or infrastructure. Ulster tenant right, as Ulster custom was also known, was formalised under the 1870 *Land-lord and Tenant (Ireland) Act* (<u>33 & 34 Vict. c. 46</u>).

unconscious cerebration The mental processes of a brain otherwise occupied which lead, nonetheless, to logically correct conclusions such as might be produced by conscious thought. The concept was developed by the **physician** William Benjamin Carpenter (1813–85) from 1853.

underground railways The world's first underground **railway** system, the Metropolitan Railway, was opened in London in 1863, as a private enterprise. This, and subsequent lines built by other railway companies in the English capital, were worked by steam locomotives until the deployment of reliable electric traction from 1890. Outside of London, a short underground railway connected Liverpool and Birkenhead from 1886, and a circular subway was opened in Glasgow in 1896.

undertaker An individual or company which 'undertook' to organise all aspects of a funeral including (potentially) the purchase of the grave, coffin and memorial; the transport of the deceased and the mourners from church to cemetery; the employment of **mutes** and provision of **feather trays**; and the conduct of the first stages of a ritual **mourning** which often extended long after the day of interment. See also: **cremation; mourning stationery; mourning warehouse.**

Union Flag The national flag of the United Kingdom, which embodies the red cross of St George (England), the white saltire of St Andrew (Scotland) and the red saltire of St Patrick (Ireland), which dates from 1801. The heraldic insignia of Wales – the red dragon – does not appear on the flag as a consequence of the annexation of the Principality by England in 1283. The often misapplied term 'Union Jack' denotes the flag when flown at the bow of a ship.

Union Jack See: **Union Flag.**

Unionist A member of a political grouping, comprised of members of both the **Conservative** and **Liberal** parties (the latter known as **Liberal Unionists**), which opposed Irish **Home Rule**. In British usage, subscribers to **trades unions** are denominated 'trades unionists' rather than merely 'unionists'. More broadly, the term 'unionist' may theoretically be associated with an attachment to the Union with respect to all or any of the component countries of the United Kingdom, though the specific term 'Ulster Unionist' should be applied only in the contexts of British and Irish politics immediately prior to and following the partition of Ireland in 1921.

Unitarian A member of a **nonconformist** Christian denomination whose doctrines are based on the teaching of the Early Church, and whose adherents do not accept the mainstream belief in the Holy Trinity wherein God is perceived as, simultaneously, Father, Son and Holy Ghost.

universities University education at the start of the nineteenth century was conducted exclusively through a small number of ancient (and often collegiate) institutions, namely the Universities of Oxford (the oldest English institution, though formally **chartered** only in 1248), Cambridge (chartered 1231), St Andrews (founded 1413), Glasgow (founded 1451), Aberdeen (founded 1495), Edinburgh (founded 1582) and Dublin (founded 1592). Entry to these institutions was restricted by religious denomination (Oxford and Cambridge were **Anglican**, though other institutions did admit **dissenters**); by gender (women were not customarily admitted either as students or faculty); and by the ability to pay college and examination fees as well as living expenses. Demands for access to higher education by dissenters and **Roman Catholics** in the first instance led to the establishment of a number of new universities starting with Durham (founded 1832, chartered 1837) and London (chartered 1836, with King's College and University College as its first colleges). The collegiate **Queen's University of Ireland** was founded in 1845, and later expanded into the **Royal University of Ireland**; the federal **Victoria University** between 1884 and 1887; and the federal University of Wales in 1893. Though these new institutions were in most cases open to religious dissenters, non-Christians and atheists, access by women remained at best ambivalent, with female students sometimes being admitted to certain classes but not eligible to attend the examinations which determined the award of a degree. The Senate of the University of London voted to allow women to sit the General Examination in 1868. Women were not, however, awarded degrees at Oxford or Cambridge until the twentieth century, despite the foundation of exclusively female colleges such as **Girton** (1869) and **Newnham** (1871) at

Cambridge and **Somerville** and **Lady Margaret Hall** at Oxford in 1879.

university settlements An educational movement which aimed to improve the condition of the working classes, modelled upon the example of **Toynbee Hall**. University settlements were established by the faculty and student bodies of several British **universities** from the 1880s, with East London proving a particular focus and a dedicated Women's University Settlement founded as early as 1887 with support from female members of the Universities of Oxford, Cambridge and London.

uranism A euphemism for male **homosexuality**, used in particular at the **fin de siècle**.

utilitarianism A philosophical and economic doctrine based upon the premise that greatest happiness of the greatest number of people should determine social conduct. While the philosophical question of promoting a more general condition of 'happiness' ostensibly underlay the doctrine, the practicalities of applied utilitarian thought tended rather to a more basic alleviation of suffering – that is, the deployment only of the minimum economic or concrete resources required to sustain rather than significantly improve an individual's condition. This, certainly, was the central utilitarian principle which underwrote the management of many **workhouses**, as well as the charitable or institutional care exercised over those, such as the elderly or the disabled, who were unable to improve their current situation.

V

vagrancy In Victorian usage, a vagrant is an individual of either sex who lacks both a permanent residence and gainful employment, their economic precariousness rendering sporadic admission to a **workhouse** likely if not inevitable. To this definition, a moral implication was added within the **Poor Law** system whereby a distinction was drawn between ostensibly respectable working people seeking employment and the prototypically workshy habitual vagrant. Able-bodied vagrants were normally separated from the other workhouse occupants in a so-called 'casual ward', where an act of labour (such as **stone-breaking** or **oakum**-picking) would normally be required from the temporary inmate on the morning following admission. The central legislation governing the treatment of vagrants was the 1824 *Vagrancy Act* (5 Geo. 4 c. 83) and the 1882 *Casual Poor Act* (45 & 46 Vict. c. 36).

valet A male **servant** who performs duties relating to the person and dress of his employer.

VC The post-nominal abbreviation signifying possession of the **Victoria Cross**.

vegetarianism While abstaining from meat had historically been motivated by individual preference or religious belief prior to mid-century, a Vegetarian Society was founded in Ramsgate in 1847 to actively promote a meat-free diet on both ethical and health grounds. The Alpha Restaurant in Oxford Street, London, was opened in 1879 and is widely accepted as the first exclusively vegetarian establishment in Britain.

velocipede See: **bicycle**.

velveteen A fabric with a finish similar to velvet but made from inexpensive cotton rather than silk.

venereal disease The spread of sexually transmitted diseases in garrison and naval towns was policed through a combination of criminalisation and medicalisation which confined female **prostitutes** in order to protect their male clients. The *Contagious Diseases Act* of 1864 (<u>27 & 28 Vict. c. 85</u>), supplemented by further legislation in 1866 (<u>29 & 30 Vict. c. 35</u>) and 1869 (<u>32 & 33 Vict. c. 96</u>), facilitated the arrest and clinical inspection of suspected prostitutes, and authorised both the interventive treatment and incarceration of **syphilitic** women in so-called **lock hospitals**. The most effective opposition to the legislation came not from the prostitutes themselves, nor their clients, but from the educated middle-class women who founded the Ladies' National Association for the Repeal of the *Contagious Diseases Acts* in 1869. The legislation was repealed in 1886.

viceroy An individual appointed as the governor general of a colonial territory and whose actions are implicitly authorised by the Crown, though directed by government policy. In British imperial practice, viceroys were usually appointed from the **peerage** or the military and participated in local ceremonial duties (such as investitures and anniversaries) as the representative of the monarch.

view halloo A phrase shouted aloud while **hunting** to signify that a fox has broken cover and is visible in the open.

Victoria Cross The highest award in the nineteenth century for gallantry while engaged in military or naval action, the **VC** was instituted in 1856 following the **Crimean War**. The medal was reputedly cast from captured Russian cannons, and suspended from a crimson or dark-blue ribbon to denote a military or naval recipient respectively.

Victoria Street Society See: vivisection.

Victoria University A federal **university**, formed in 1880, with Owens College – a non-sectarian institution founded in Manchester in 1851 – as its first constituent body, followed by University College, Liverpool (founded 1881), and Yorkshire College, Leeds, in 1887. Liverpool and Leeds separated from the Victoria University in 1903 and 1904, respectively.

Victorian sages A concept popularised by John Holloway's 1953 book, *The Victorian Sage: Studies in Argument*, and premised upon the pervasive influence of writers and thinkers whose works were contemplated, variously, as contemporary commentary, moral valorisations or prophetic warnings. Holloway's defining sages were the essayists Matthew Arnold (1822–88), Thomas Carlyle (1795–1881) and John Henry Newman (1801–90), and the novelists Benjamin Disraeli (1804–81), George Eliot (1819–80) and Thomas Hardy (1840–1928), though these might be readily supplemented with, among others, Walter Pater (1839–94), John Ruskin (1819–1900) and Samuel Smiles (1812–1904), author of *Self-Help* (1859).

vim An Americanism, incorporated into British English in the mid-nineteenth century, denoting the positive qualities of vigour or energy.

vitriol In full, oil of vitriol, a concentrated sulphuric acid, sometimes employed in violent assaults. Skin exposed to vitriol would inevitably be scarred and disfigured to a greater or lesser extent, which made vitriol-throwing a supposed weapon of choice for revenge-seeking lovers, though chemical scarring and blinding were also occasionally inflicted upon employers and strike-breaking workers during industrial disputes.

vivisection Interventive surgical – and, occasionally, chemical – experimentation upon living animals routinely formed part of the training of **surgeons** as well as the anatomical research conducted by medical professionals across the nineteenth century.

Public distaste for the practice led to the formation of the Victoria Street Society in 1875, which was renamed the National Anti-Vivisection Society in 1897, and a British Union of Anti-Vivisection Societies in 1898. Despite this organised opposition to vivisection, the practice was regulated – though still essentially protected – by the 1876 *Cruelty to Animals Act* (39 & 40 Vict. c. 77), colloquially known as the *Vivisection Act*.

volley pistol See: **mob pistol**.

VR The monogram or cypher of Queen Victoria – being the initials of the Latin equivalent, Victoria Regina – which customarily appeared (often accompanied by an image of the crown) on official documentation, military property, medals and regimental insignia, and postal collection boxes.

vril A mysterious and intangible force, which forms the subject of the futuristic novel *The Coming Race* (1871) by Edward Bulwer Lytton (1803–73). The beef extract Bovril was punningly named as such in 1886, and prefaced the name of Lytton's force with a contracted form of the word 'bovine' – the Latin term for cattle and oxen.

W

wallah Derived from the Hindi, a term initially deployed in India as a suffix to define indigenous labour – **chai-wallah**, **punkah-wallah** – but later extended to colloquial descriptions of British individuals at home or in colonial context, most notably **box-wallah**.

Waterloo Cup, the First organised at Altcar near Liverpool in 1836 by the proprietor of the **Grand National**, the most prestigious annual **hare-coursing** event in Britain.

Waterloo teeth Dentures made from extracted human teeth, often set into an ivory palate or gum. The teeth were sourced primarily from dead bodies, the name recalling how many were taken from corpses on the field of Waterloo (1815), including those exhumed by **resurrection men**, though paid living donors were occasionally utilised. See also: **gutta percha**.

wet bob An individual – almost invariably a gentleman – who devotes their spare time to water-based activities such as rowing or sailing. The term originated within the **public school** system, most likely at Eton College, and gained currency amongst university undergraduates and young professionals across the century. A dry bob, by contrast, favoured land-based sports such as **cricket** or **rugby football**.

whaling An important activity in commercial fishing. Whaling vessels based at domestic ports such as Whitby and Aberdeen hunted and part-processed whales while still at sea in order to obtain the blubber and **spermaceti** from which fats and oils were produced for industrial and domestic use. Flexible whalebone, suitable for **stays** and **corsets**, was a further by-product of this process. British whaling in the southern hemisphere was negligible for much of the nineteenth century, but was developed from a base at Grytviken in the Falkland Islands from 1904.

Whig See: **Liberal Party**.

whip In both the **House of Commons** and **House of Lords**, a regular member of the legislature who both publicises and enforces the party line when members vote on a measure under debate. The term also refers to the formal allegiance of a member to his party: the whip may thus be 'withdrawn' punitively from a member who fails to vote with the government on a specific piece of legislature.

whipper-in In **hunting**, an assistant to the huntsman responsible for returning straying hounds to the pack.

whist A popular card-game for four players, playing in pairs, which frequently formed part of an evening's social entertainment in middle- and upper-class homes. **Bridge** is a development of whist.

Whitechapel Murders A series of violent attacks in which five – or possibly six – women were mutilated and murdered in the East End of London in 1888. The attribution of the murders to a single perpetrator – **Jack the Ripper** – is questionable, and the number of deaths has similarly been disputed. Wide publicity in the popular media prompted not merely a contemplation of the extent of **prostitution** and social deprivation in the capital city but also a rise in anti-Semitism, with the perpetrator being identified by some as a Jewish slaughterman and by others as a mentally unstable **surgeon** or **physician**.

Who's Who First published in 1849 as a short almanac that also incorporated lists of ranks and appointments within the Royal Household, the **House of Commons** and **House of Lords**, and the **Anglican** Church, *Who's Who* expanded into a significant resource of detailed information when, in 1897, it began to include short autobiographical statements provided by a wider range of public figures.

widow's weeds The black garments characteristically worn by a woman in **mourning** for her deceased husband.

Wisden In full, *Wisden Cricketers' Almanack*, an annual publication, independent of the governing body of **cricket**, first issued in 1864.

workhouse Under the **Poor Law**, a locally funded institution in which the destitute – and often also the physically and mentally ill – were accommodated under a system of **indoor relief**. Workhouse conditions were characteristically harsh, in order to deter the admission of those physically able to work, and were usually structured around the separation of families and segregation of the sexes, menial and physically hard tasks such as **stone-breaking** and **oakum-picking**, and a plain and meagre diet often based upon coarse bread and **gruel**.

worsted A smooth fabric spun from wool.

writer to the Signet In Scots legal usage, a solicitor.

X

X-rays Accidentally discovered in 1895 by Wilhelm Röntgen (1845–1923), and initially named in his honour, X-ray technology was first illustrated in Britain by Archibald Campbell Swinton (1863–1930), who published a photograph of the bones of his hand in the journal *Nature* on 23 January 1896. The technology was deployed in British hospital practice as early as 1896, X-rays having an obvious application in the early diagnosis of **tuberculosis**, and a dedicated Röntgen Society was formed in London in 1897.

Y

yellow A significant colour within British **fin-de-siècle** culture, yellow conventionally denoted the presence of **decadence** in the literature and art of its adherents, while for those who saw such posturing as degenerate, it connoted the languor and sickness of an **Aestheticism** typified by oriental and **greenery-yallary** decoration. Yellow was the favoured colour for the covers of works whose content might be regarded with some suspicion – as well as the yellow-covered (and possibly French) novel that is pointedly referenced in *The Picture of Dorian Gray* (1890) by Oscar Wilde (1854–1900), *Dracula* (1897) by Bram Stoker (1847–1912) was published between yellow boards, as was the aptly titled **Yellow Book**.

Yellow Book, The A quarterly periodical, published between 1894 and 1897, which positioned literature and art as cultural equals within its pages, and garnered a sometimes-negative reputation as the foremost British exemplar of cultural **decadence** and **Aestheticism**. Its literary contributors included Henry James (1843–1916), Richard Le Gallienne (1866–1947) and the pseudonymous **New Woman** writer George Egerton (1859–1945), while its graphic content – which was edited by Aubrey Beardsley (1872–98) – was provided by, among others, Max Beerbohm (1872–1956) and Walter Sickert (1860–1942).

yeomanry A volunteer cavalry force, which operated parallel to the **militia**.

Young Men's Christian Association Founded in London in 1844 in order to provide lower-middle-class urban males with an alternative to the temptations of **music hall**, alcohol and premarital sexual dalliance, the YMCA afforded a wholesome regime of Bible study, instructive lectures and reading rooms later supplemented by organised holidays and physical exercise on the model of *mens sana in corpore sano*. The movement attained a global reach as early as 1855.

Z

zoetrope An optical device which employs a rotating cylinder with a series of illustrations on its inner surface to give the impression of a moving picture when these are viewed through a series of slits positioned on its vertical plane.

Zulu A member of a Bantu people who occupied land in KwaZulu-Natal Province, South Africa. The Zulus resisted European colonisation, opposing the **Boers** in 1838 and the British in a series of Zulu Wars between 1879 and 1897, these including a significant victory against the British at Islandwana in 1879 and the unsuccessful attack upon Rorke's Drift (KwaJimu), following which the **Victoria Cross** was awarded to eleven surviving British servicemen. Cetshwayo kaMpande (1826–84), King of the Zulus (1873–9), was exiled first to Cape Town and then to London following the defeat of his nation, gaining considerable public sympathy in the latter location. As Cetywayo, he was referenced by the imperial novelist H. Rider Haggard (1856-1925) in two Victorian fictions, *The Witch's Head* (1885) and *Black Heart and White Heart* (1900), and discussed in political context in *Cetywayo and His White Neighbours* (1882).

Figure 29 Queen Victoria, photographed by Alexander Bassano (1882).

A Chronology of the Reign of Queen Victoria

(24 May 1819–22 January 1901)

1819   Alexandrina Victoria born on 24 May at Kensington Palace, London.

1837   Accession of Queen Victoria on 20 June; coronation on 28 June 1838; opening of first London **railway** terminus at Euston; serial publication of Dickens's *Oliver Twist* begins; effective abolition of **slavery** in the British colonies with compensation to former slave owners.

1838   Formulation of the People's Charter; Grand Junction **Railway** between London and Birmingham opens.

1839   **Whig** prime minister Viscount Melbourne resigns, but returns to office when Sir Robert Peel declines to form a **Tory** government; **Chartist** petition presented to Parliament but rejected; soldiers fire on Chartists in Newport, Wales; Anti-**Corn Law** League formed; first **Opium War** begins.

1840   Parliament authorises local **Poor Law** authorities to provide vaccination for the poor funded by ratepayers. Treaty of Waitangi incorporates New Zealand into the British Empire; Queen Victoria marries Prince Albert of Saxe-Coburg-Gotha; introduction of the **Penny Post**.

1841   Sir Robert Peel forms a **Conservative** government; *Punch* launched; Hong Kong ceded to the British following the first **Opium War**.

1842   **Income tax** reintroduced by Peel's administration; second **Chartist** petition rejected by Parliament; Webster–Ashburton Treaty fixes US–Canadian border; three separate attempts are made to assassinate Queen Victoria.

1843   Schism within the Scottish **Kirk**; William Wordsworth succeeds Robert Southey as **poet laureate**; a **Rebecca riot** destroys the Carmarthen **workhouse**; British forces annex the Indian province of Sind.

1844   **Young Men's Christian Association** established; the **Rochdale Pioneers** open the first co-operative shop.

1845   Nationwide **Protestant** anger following the granting of government funds to the **Roman Catholic** Maynooth College, County Kildare; **Tractarian** John Henry Newman converts to **Roman Catholicism**; potato blight appears in Ireland at the same time as poor harvests elsewhere in Britain; Robert Peel tenders his resignation as prime minister, which the Queen refuses.

1846   **Potato famine** in Ireland and the Scottish Highlands; Edwin Chadwick reveals the depth of urban social deprivation in **Poor Law** Commission report; Treaty of Lahore ends conflict between British and Sikh forces in India; **Corn Laws** are repealed; **Conservative** prime minister Robert Peel resigns and is replaced by the **Whig** Lord John Russell.

1847   The *Factories Act* (10 & 11 Vict. c. 29) – known as the 'Ten Hour Act' – restricts working day for women and children; the continuing **potato famine**, epidemic fever and poverty in Ireland provoke mass emigration; serial publication of *Vanity Fair* by William Makepeace Thackeray; pseudonymous **triple-decker** publication of *Jane Eyre* and *Wuthering Heights* by Charlotte and Emily Brontë, respectively.

1848   The year of political revolutions in Europe; Karl Marx and Friedrich Engels publish *The Communist Manifesto* in German; significant **Chartist** agitation in London and Glasgow; **potato famine** in highland Scotland begins a second wave of emigration; **cholera** epidemic prompts local and central government to intervene in the interests of public health.

1849   **Chartist** petition rejected by Parliament; **cholera** epidemic continues; the Punjab is annexed to British-ruled India; sectarian violence breaks out between **Orangemen** and **Roman Catholics** at Dolly's Brae, Castlewellan/Magheramayo; the **Queen's University of Ireland** is established by Royal Charter; **Pre-Raphaelite** Brotherhood initiated.

1850   Alfred Tennyson appointed **poet laureate**; the Don Pacifico Affair; the *Party Processions Act* is passed in part as a response to the 1849 skirmish at Dolly's Brae; Pope Pius IX authorises re-establishment of **Roman Catholic** hierarchy in England and Wales, provoking **Protestant** anger both outside and within Parliament.

1851   The **Great Exhibition** opens in Hyde Park; *The Ecclesiastical Titles Act* (14 & 15 Vict. c. 60) is passed in response to Pope Pius IX's actions in 1850; a Catholic Defence Association is formed to oppose the act; a gold rush begins in New South Wales, Australia. Lord Palmerston, who supported the 1851 coup in France, is dismissed as foreign secretary; a census of church attendance in England and Wales reveals both a decline in **Anglican** observance and a significant number of people who attended no religious service at all.

1852   Lord John Russell resigns as prime minister, to be replaced in February by the Earl of Derby as the leader of a **Tory** minority government including Benjamin Disraeli as chancellor of the exchequer; Derby's ministry is succeeded in December by an effective coalition under the **Conservative** Earl of Aberdeen, with William Ewart Gladstone (then a Conservative) as chancellor of the exchequer and Palmerston (**Whig**) as home secretary; Britain recognises the independence of the Transvaal **Boers** under the Sand River Convention; British troops seize Rangoon, prior to the annexation of Burma; the Duke of Wellington dies, aged eighty-four; the troopship HMS *Birkenhead* sinks off the coast of South Africa, the reputed survival of all of the women and children on board passing into popular mythology as an exemplification of modern British chivalry.

1853   British naval fleet despatched to the Dardanelles to counter Russian ambitions in the Ottoman Empire; the Ottoman Empire declares war on Russia and suffers defeat at sea; **transportation** to Australia ends; the *Public Houses Act* (16 & 17 Vict. c. 67) closes public houses in Scotland between 11 p.m. and 8 a.m. on weekdays and all day on Sunday; mandatory vaccination of children against smallpox is introduced in England and Wales; Prince Albert orders the renovation and extension of Balmoral House, creating a public fashion for **Balmorality**.

1854   Britain and France declare war on Russia on 26 March, landing in the Crimea on 13 September; John Snow links the spread of **cholera** to contaminated water supplies; cholera begins to spread amongst troops fighting in the **Crimean War**; the Charge of the Light Brigade takes place on 25 October.

1855   The Aberdeen administration falls, in part over the conduct of the **Crimean War**; Palmerston forms a **Whig** administration; Russian-occupied Sebastopol (now called Sevastopol) surrenders to allied forces following a siege lasting almost a year; David Livingstone discovers Victoria Falls; the London sewer system is modernised, in part to prevent further outbreaks of **cholera**; Tennyson publishes *Maud, and Other Poems*.

1856   The **Crimean War** formally concludes with the Treaty of Paris; regional and provincial **police** forces are formed across the United Kingdom; British gunboats attack Chinese fortifications guarding Canton (now Guangzhou) following an incident in which a Hong Kong-based vessel had been seized.

1857   Palmerston calls and wins a general election, following parliamentary condemnation of his support for 'gunboat diplomacy' in China; an uprising by **sepoy** troops based at Meerut starts the **Indian Mutiny**; the *Matrimonial Causes Act* (20 & 21 Vict. c. 85) permits **divorce**, but on terms that favour male over female litigants; the *Obscene Publications Act* (20 & 21 Vict. c. 83) is passed; Thomas Hughes publishes *Tom Brown's Schooldays*.

1858   Irish Republican Brotherhood founded; Lionel de Rothschild becomes first Jewish MP; Lord Derby becomes **Conservative** prime minister; abolition of the East India Company through the *Government of India Act* (21 & 22 Vict. c. 106); **Indian Mutiny** ends; Treaty of Tientsin ostensibly ends a period of Anglo-Chinese conflict, but is not ratified by China.

1859   Charles Darwin's *On the Origin of Species by Means of Natural Selection* sold out in advance of its launch; Lord Derby's **Conservative** administration collapses, to be succeeded by a **Whig** government under Viscount Palmerston; Samuel Smiles publishes *Self-Help*.

1860   HMS *Warrior*, the first British iron-framed and iron-clad battleship is launched; British and French troops take Beijing, the **Opium Wars** being formally ended with the Treaty of Beijing and five 'treaty ports' (including Shanghai) being opened to

British traders through the ratification of the 1858 Treaty of Tientsin; the theory of **evolution**, popularised by Charles Darwin, is debated by clergy and scientists at the Oxford Union; work begins on the first **underground railway** in London.

1861   Civil war begins in the United States, with Britain declaring a policy of neutrality; Queen Victoria and Albert, **Prince Consort** make a state visit to Ireland in August; **savings banks** for the low-paid are proposed as part of the existing national Post Office system; Prince Albert dies of **typhus** on 15 December.

1862   CSS *Alabama*, built at Birkenhead for the Confederate States of America, despite British neutrality in the ongoing US Civil War; the construction of **Albertopolis**, a district of public buildings designed as a memorial to the **Prince Consort**, begins opposite Hyde Park, London; the Peabody Trust is formed in London in order to build affordable and sanitary accommodation for the low-paid; a sectarian riot takes place in Hyde Park on 5 October, provoked by domestic **Protestant** support for the Italian politician Giuseppe Garibaldi (1807–82).

1863   The Metropolitan Line is opened as London's first **underground railway**; Broadmoor Asylum for the criminally insane opens in Berkshire, taking inmates from across the country; the **Prince of Wales** marries Princess Alexandra of Denmark; Charles Kingsley (1819–75) publishes *The Water Babies*, a Christian fairy tale; the rules of **association football** are formally codified.

1864   The **Peabody Trust** opens its first housing estate for the poor in Spitalfields, London; Giuseppe Garibaldi visits London in April and meets the **Prince of Wales**; the International Working Men's Association (popularly known as the 'First International') is founded in London with the support of British **trades unionists** and foreign intellectuals, including Karl Marx (1818–83); the *Contagious Diseases Act* (27 & 28 Vict. c. 85) is introduced in order to restrict the spread of **venereal disease** in military and naval centres by suppressing **prostitution**; the *Penal Servitude Amendment Act* (27 & 28 Vict. c. 47) sets minimum-sentence tariffs for first and repeat offences, and requires **ticket-of-leave** holders to report to the **police** each month.

1865   An uprising occurs at Morant Bay in Jamaica, which is violently suppressed by the colonial governor, Edward John Eyre (1815–1901); Lord Palmerston dies and is succeeded as **Whig** prime minister by John, Lord Russell (1792–1878); the *Prisons Act* introduces harsher custodial sentences including provisions for separate confinement, **hard labour** and dietary restrictions for prisoners.

1866   American **Fenians** attempt to invade the island of Campo Bello, near Maine, in April and Canada in June; Parliament suspends *habeas corpus* in Ireland; **cholera** epidemic in London; electoral agitation in Hyde Park, London; Russell's administration collapses over the franchise, to be succeeded by a minority **Conservative** government headed by Lord Derby in the **House of Lords** with Benjamin Disraeli leading the party in the **House of Commons**.

1867   The *British North America Act* creates an almost completely self-governing Dominion of Canada; the final convict ship carrying British and Irish prisoners sentenced to **transportation** sails for Australia; **Fenians** stage an unsuccessful uprising in Ireland and fail to capture the arsenal of Chester Castle in England; separate attempts to rescue Fenian prisoners from captivity in Manchester and London lead to police and civilian fatalities; women's suffrage is raised in Parliament during the debate surrounding the *Representation of the People Act* (30 & 31 Vict. c. 102) – the so-called 'Second **Reform Act**'; mandatory vaccination against smallpox is extended to all children under the age of fourteen; Joseph Lister demonstrates antiseptic surgery using carbolic acid.

1868   Elizabeth Lynn Linton's anti-feminist essay 'The Girl of the Period' appears in the *Saturday Review*; a sectarian riot takes place in Ashton-under-Lyne, Lancashire; the last **public execution** takes place at the Old Bailey, London; the first meeting of the National Society for Women's Suffrage takes place in Manchester; Disraeli succeeds Derby as **Conservative** prime minister, but is defeated by the **Liberal** Gladstone in a November general election; **Trades Union Congress** organised in Manchester.

1869   Gladstone's *Irish Church Act* (32 & 33 Vict. c. 42) authorises **disestablishment** of the **Anglican** Church in Ireland from 1871; John Stuart Mill publishes *The Subjection of Women* which argues for female equality and emancipation; Parliament passes the *Municipal Franchise Act* which granted female ratepayers the right to vote in local elections; Matthew Arnold publishes *Culture and Anarchy*; Sophia Jex-Blake (1840–1912) and six other women matriculate as medical students at Edinburgh University, creating a precedent for female access to higher education; concerns regarding public health provoke the passing of a further **Contagious Diseases Act** (32 & 33 Vict. c. 96), which proves controversial.

1870   The **Married Women's Property Act** (33 & 34 Vict. c. 93) allows women to maintain a greater control over inherited property, investments and earnings; Britain declares neutrality in the Franco-Prussian War; Isaac Butt (1813–79) founds the Home Government Association to campaign for Irish Home Rule; the *Landlord and Tenant (Ireland) Act* changes the relationship between the two parties in an Irish tenancy, changing the law regarding eviction in particular; a telegraph cable is opened between Britain and India; the *Elementary Education Act* (33 & 34 Vict. c. 75) – popularly known as 'Forster's Education Act' – expands the provision of elementary education in England.

1871   The *Trades Union Act* (34 & 35 Vict. c. 31) grants legal recognition to trades unions, but maintains significant restrictions with regard to picketing and strike action; the **Bank Holidays Act** (34 & 35 Vict c. 17) authorises four additional days each year on which commercial business is not customarily transacted; annexation of Griqualand in Southern Africa by Britain, prompting an expansion in diamond prospecting in the region; the Treaty of London attempts to stabilise international law by regularising the conditions by which a nation might withdraw from an agreement between powers; the Prince of Wales recovers from typhoid fever.

1872   Gladstone makes his first speech in the House of Commons in support of Irish Home Rule; the *Education (Scotland) Act* (35 & 36 Vict. c. 62) makes attendance at school compulsory for children between the ages of five and thirteen; the National Agricultural Labourers' Union is founded; the *Ballot Act* (35 & 36 Vict. c. 33) ends the historic practice of open voting; the pro-temperance *Licensing Act* (35 & 36 Vict c. 94) proves unpopular in working-class areas and is viewed by some public figures as an attack on individual freedom; the first **university** college in Wales opens at Aberystwyth.

1873   Gladstone resigns as **Liberal** prime minister in March following the defeat of the Irish **University** Bill but returns to office six days later, Disraeli having refused to form a minority **Conservative** administration; the **Home Rule** League is founded in Dublin; a British military force is despatched in December to the Gold Coast (now Ghana) under Sir Garnet Wolseley, leading to war with the Ashanti under King Kofi Kari-Kari.

1874   Gladstone asks for Parliament to be dissolved in January; the **Conservatives** return to power under Disraeli in February; in the new Parliament two miners are elected to Parliament with **Liberal** support, one of whom expresses support for **temperance**; the Ashanti War ends in March; the *Factory Act* (37 & 38 Vict. c. 44) enforced a maximum working day of ten hours on weekdays in textile factories with a shorter day on Saturday and initiated the process through which the employment of children in mills was gradually ended; Girton College is established at Cambridge to provide **university** level education for women; the *Public Worship Regulation Act* (37 & 38 Vict. c. 85) is passed as a **Protestant** response to **ritualism** and the **Oxford Movement**.

1875   The *Conspiracy and Protection of Property Act* (38 & 39 Vict. c. 86) legalises strike action and picketing by **trades unions**; the *Public Health Act* brings sanitation under local authority oversight in the interests of preventing **epidemics** as well as improving general public hygiene; the *Artisans' and Labourers' Dwellings Improvement Act* 1875 (38 & 39 Vict. c. 36) empowered local authorities to purchase dwellings in the interest of slum clearance; Newnham College is founded at Cambridge as a **university** level institution for women; Disraeli purchases a controlling interest in the **Suez Canal**, securing a safe and rapid sea route to India via the Mediterranean and the Red Sea.

1876   The *Royal Titles Bill* (39 & 40 Vict. c. 10) adds the denomination 'Empress of India' to the formal title of Queen Victoria; reports reach England of massacres and other atrocities committed by Turkish irregular soldiers in Bulgaria, with Gladstone highlighting the matter in a pamphlet entitled

The Bulgarian Horrors and the Question of the East; a **Home Rule** motion proposed by Isaac Butt is defeated in the **House of Commons**; the *Elementary Education Act* (39 & 40 Vict. c. 79) further enhanced the provision of universal basic education through the payment of school fees and further restrictions upon the employment of children; Disraeli is raised to the **peerage** under the title of Earl of Beaconsfield by Queen Victoria and leads the **Conservative** government from the **House of Lords**.

1877   Britain declares neutrality in the Russo-Turkish War; Britain annexes the **Boer** Transvaal Republic; Charles Stewart Parnell (1846–91) replaces Isaac Butt as the acknowledged leader of the Irish **Home Rule** movement; John Ruskin (1819–1900) describes the radical *Nocturne* paintings of James Abbott McNeill Whistler (1834–1903), exhibited at the **Grosvenor Galley**, as a 'wilful imposture' on the public; Annie Besant (1847–1933) and Charles Bradlaugh (1833–91) are prosecuted for issuing a pamphlet encouraging the use of contraception: the trial proves inconclusive.

1878   The defeat of the Turkish Empire and consolidation of Russian influence in the Balkans threatens British power in the Mediterranean and unhindered access to the **Suez Canal**; the subsequent Congress of Berlin adjusts the balance, limiting Russian ambitions and restoring some of the provinces displaced by the Turkish defeat; the Christian Mission, founded in 1865, changes its name to the **Salvation Army**; the *Factory and Workshop Act* (41 & 42 Vict. c. 16) consolidated several earlier acts into a single piece of legislation, regulating the length of the working week and the employment of minors, and extending regulations to a wider range of industrial activities – but *not* to agriculture or mining.

1879   **Zulu** forces defeat British and indigenous troops at Isandhlwana (now Isandlwana), but fail to overrun the garrison at Rorke's Drift; Michael Davitt (1846–1906) forms the **Irish National Land League** with Parnell as president; the Tay **railway** bridge collapses during a storm, killing at least fifty-nine people; Gladstone begins to campaign in Midlothian in pursuit of a third term as prime minister.

1880   Disraeli requests a dissolution of Parliament in March, and Gladstone's **Liberals** win the subsequent election; Charles

Bradlaugh, elected MP for Northampton, refuses to take the oath of office on account of his atheism; the **Irish National Land League** initiates a campaign of **boycotting** in County Mayo, and **Orangemen** from County Cavan are recruited, with protection from the police and military, to harvest the crops; the port of Liverpool is granted city status.

1881   Parnell is suspended from the **House of Commons** following an obstructionist intervention into a debate on the reintroduction of **coercion** into Ireland; the *Land Law (Ireland) Act* (44 & 45 Vict. c. 49) stabilises rents and ostensibly encourages the purchase of land by tenants; amid rent strikes and other acts of disruption, the **Irish National Land League** is outlawed by Parliament, and Parnell, with other members of the organisation, is imprisoned; the **Boers** defeat British troops at Majuba Hill.

1882   The so-called 'Kilmainham Treaty' sees Parnell and his associates released from gaol on 2 May in the interests of quelling agrarian unrest in Ireland; four days later the chief secretary and the permanent under-secretary for Ireland are assassinated in Phoenix Park, Dublin; the **Irish National League** is formed as a successor to the outlawed land League; violence breaks out on the Isle of Skye between tenants and landlords over evictions and the removal of long-held tenancies – a Highland Land League is formed in 1883; the **Anglican** Church founds the **Church Army** on the model of the **Salvation Army**; a second *Married Women's Property Act* grants married women essentially the same rights over their assets as spinsters.

1883   Five members of the **Invincibles** – an Irish nationalist organisation – are found guilty of the Phoenix Park Murders and sentenced to death; British forces suffer significant losses in the Sudan during a religiously defined conflict, the Mahdist War; the *Corrupt and Illegal Practices Prevention Act* (46 & 47 Vict. c. 51) defines the role of election agents and limits expenses; the *Cheap Trains Act* (46 & 47 Vict. c. 34) removes the tax on low-price workmen's **railway** tickets and encourages railway companies to provide cheaper trains for workers; the **Boys' Brigade** is formed in Glasgow.

1884   The National Society for the Prevention of Cruelty to Children (NSPCC) is founded – an Irish equivalent is founded in 1889; the **University** of Oxford passes a statute which permits women to sit examinations; Parliament passes the *Representation of the People Act* (48 & 49 Vict. c. 3) – the so-called 'Third **Reform Act'**; Alfred Tennyson (1809–92), the **poet laureate**, is raised to the **peerage** by Queen Victoria; the Gaelic Athletic Association (GAA) is formed in Ireland to preserve indigenous sports in the context of an Irish – rather than British – cultural milieu; General Gordon is despatched to the Sudan to evacuate British troops from Khartoum, which is besieged by Mahdist troops.

1885   General Gordon is killed at Khartoum before a relief expedition under Wolseley is able to reach the city; Gladstone is subsequently vilified in the popular press for delaying authorisation of the relief force; **Fenians** plant bombs at the Tower of London and **House of Commons**; the Society for Utilising the Welsh Language is founded to preserve the traditional language of Wales; the Irish Loyal and Patriotic Union is formed in Dublin to counter the **Home Rule** movement; Gladstone resigns as prime minister following the defeat of his budget in the House of Commons, and is succeeded by Lord Salisbury (1830–1903) leading a minority **Conservative** administration whose ability to govern depends upon the assistance of Parnell and his colleagues; William Thomas Stead (1849–1912), editor of the *Pall Mall Gazette*, is prosecuted for ostensibly abducting a minor while exposing the extent of child prostitution in London.

1886   Cymru Fydd and the Scottish **Home Rule** Association are founded to campaign for Home Rule in Wales and Scotland, respectively; Britain annexes Upper Burma (now Myanmar); Salisbury resigns as his government is defeated to be replaced by Gladstone; the *Shop Hours Regulation Act* (49 & 50 Vict. c. 55) limits the working hours of minors working in the retail trade; the *Contagious Diseases Acts* are repealed; the *Pall Mall Gazette* publishes allegations regarding an adulterous relationship between Parnell and Mrs Katherine ('Kitty') O'Shea (1846–1921); parliamentary business is dominated by Home Rule, with Gladstone introducing a bill (which is rejected) in June; Salisbury and the **Conservatives** return to power in July with **Liberal Unionist** support.

1887   The Golden **Jubilee** of Queen Victoria's reign; the first conference of the self-governing colonies takes place in London; Britain signs treaties with Italy and Austria-Hungary to safeguard its interests in the Mediterranean; a scarlet fever **epidemic** breaks out in London; *The Times* publishes allegations which link Parnell to the 1882 Phoenix Park Murders: the letters on which they are based are exposed as forgeries in 1889; police and military forces deploy force against Irish demonstrators on **Bloody Sunday**.

1888   The Scottish Labour Party is founded as a socialist organisation; Britain declares the establishment of two successive protectorates in Borneo; the **Whitechapel Murders** take place; Annie Besant (1847–1933) publicises the situation of the female employees at the Bryant and May match factory: the 'matchgirls' strike for twelve days; the *Local Government Act* (51 & 52 Vict. c. 41) establishes new county councils and county boroughs in England and Wales.

1889   The *Indecent Advertisements Act* (52 & 53 Vict. c. 18) criminalises the 'obscene' advertising of publications or services relating to sexuality or **venereal diseases**; three women are elected to the London County Council; the Plumage League is founded by Emily Williamson (1855–1936) to oppose the use of feathers in **millinery** – it becomes the Society for the Protection of Birds in 1891, gaining the prefix Royal in 1904; Captain William O'Shea files a **divorce** petition, openly naming Parnell as an adulterer.

1890   The *Pall Mall Gazette* calls for the resignation of Parnell as leader of the Irish parliamentary party due to his involvement in the O'Shea **divorce** case; Parnell's moral indiscretion divides the Irish party into two factions and alienates the **Liberal Party**; Cecil John Rhodes (1853–1902) becomes prime minister of Cape Colony in Southern Africa; William Booth (1829–1912), founder of the **Salvation Army**, publishes *In Darkest England and the Way Out*, a study of urban poverty in London; the *Housing of the Working Classes Act* (53 & 54 Vict. c. 70) consolidates a number of existing measures associated with slum housing but provides no financial support for improvement.

1891   The *Elementary Education Act* (54 & 55 Vict. c. 56) makes basic education free for all families in England and Wales by way of a subsidy from central government of ten **shillings** a year per child; the **Prince of Wales** is implicated in a **baccarat** scandal and subsequently appears in court as a witness; a submarine **telephone** cable links London and Paris; the **Liberal Party** becomes irretrievably divided over the issue of **Home Rule**, the **Liberal Unionists** under Joseph Chamberlain (1836–1914) aligning themselves to the **Conservatives** with regard to this and some other policies; William Morris establishes the Kelmscott Press, on **Arts and Crafts** principles, in Oxfordshire.

1892   A meeting of 12,000 **Unionists** and **Liberal Unionists** takes place in Belfast; James Keir Hardie (1856–1915) is elected as the first independent Labour MP; Gladstone forms his fourth **Liberal** administration, with the co-operation of Irish MPs, with a commitment to **Home Rule**; the provision of free and compulsory **elementary education** is extended to Ireland.

1893   An Independent Labour Party is formed by Hardie and two other socialist MPs; the introduction of a second **Home Rule** bill provokes sectarian rioting in Belfast; the Home Rule Bill is approved by the **House of Commons** but rejected by the **House of Lords**; the Gaelic League is founded to revive the Irish language and further develop a discrete cultural identity for Ireland; Rhodes extends the influence of his British South Africa Company into Matabele country by deploying British forces; the federal **University** of Wales is formally chartered.

1894   Gladstone resigns as **Liberal** prime minister to be replaced by the Earl of Rosebery (1847–1929); the *Local Government Act* (56 & 57 Vict. c. 73) permits women to vote and serve on **parish**, rural district and urban district councils; the *Finance Act* (56 & 57 Vict. c. 30) imposes estate duties (colloquially called 'death duties') as a tax on inheritance; the first issue of the *Yellow Book* is published.

1895   Oscar Wilde (1854–1900) is imprisoned for two years with **hard labour** following a trial which demonised **homosexuality** in England; Rosebery resigns to be replaced by the **Conservative** Lord Salisbury; the three Independent Labour Party candidates lose their seats in the same election; Henry Irving (1838–1905) becomes the first actor be granted a knighthood; the **Jameson Raid** takes place; the National Trust is founded in order to 'promote the permanent preservation for the benefit of the Nation of lands and tenements (including buildings) of beauty or historic interest'.

1896   Rhodes resigns as prime minister of Cape colony following his perceived complicity in the **Jameson Raid**; the *Agricultural Rates Act* (59 & 60 Vict. c. 16) reduces the burden of local taxation upon farmers, and is in part a response to the reduction in profitability prompted by the import of cheap grain; the 1865 *Locomotive Act* (28 & 29 Vict. c. 83) and subsequent legislation known colloquially as the 'Red Flag Acts' are repealed, permitting motor vehicles to travel at more than 4 mph (c. 6.5 km/h) without the accompaniment of a red flag carried in advance as a warning of their presence; the British Museum and other cultural venues open on Sunday for the first time.

1897   The Diamond **Jubilee** of Queen Victoria is celebrated with church services, military and naval ceremonies, and a gathering of imperial leaders, citizens and troops in London; a colonial conference is held in parallel to the celebrations; the poem 'Recessional' by Rudyard Kipling (1865–1936) expresses unease with regard to the endurance of British imperial power; the punitive Benin Expedition burns the city of Benin in Nigeria and appropriates the so-called 'Benin Bronzes', many of which are later displayed in the British Museum; a fast steam-turbine vessel is demonstrated at **Spithead**; the Automobile Club of Great Britain is founded, becoming the Royal Automobile Club (RAC) in 1907.

1898   The compulsory administration of smallpox vaccinations to children imposed through legislation in 1853 and 1867 is removed; the *Local Government (Ireland) Act* (61 & 62 Vict. c. 37) modifies the existing county system of governance and facilitates a limited enhancement in both female suffrage and qualification for elected office; an Anglo-Egyptian army under Horatio Herbert Kitchener (1850–1916) defeats Sudanese forces at Omdurman and subsequently prepares to engage with a French-led expedition at Fashoda before the latter withdraws; the New Territories are added to Hong Kong under a ninety-nine-year lease from China, greatly expanding the land under British control in the region.

1899   War breaks out between Britain and the **Boers** in Southern Africa; Mafeking (now Mahikeng) and Kimberley in Cape Colony and Ladysmith in Natal are besieged by Boer forces; British forces suffer defeats at Magersfontein in Cape Colony and Colenso in Natal; Kitchener and Lord Roberts (1832–1914) are despatched to Southern Africa to restore the British position; Ruskin College is opened in Oxford for the education of working men and women but is not affiliated to the **university**.

1900   An influenza **epidemic** breaks out in London; the sieges of Mafeking and Ladysmith end; Britain annexes the Orange Free State in Southern Africa, a former ally of the **Boers**; British forces intervene to relieve a group of Europeans besieged in Beijing during the Boxer Rebellion; the **Conservative Party** under Salisbury is returned to power following the so-called '**Khaki** Election' which was called following British successes in the South African War (Second Boer War): the war itself ends in 1902; the Labour Representation Committee is formed by trades unions and socialist organisations in order to secure future representation in the **House of Commons** independent of support or sponsorship from the **Liberal Party**.

1901   Queen Victoria dies at Osborne House, near Cowes, on 22 January at 6.30 p.m.

Prime Ministers of the United Kingdom of Great Britain and Ireland during the Reign of Queen Victoria

1835–41	William Lamb, 2nd Viscount Melbourne	Whig
1841–6	Sir Robert Peel, 2nd Baronet	Conservative
1846–52	Lord John Russell, 1st Earl Russell	Whig
1852	Edward Smith Stanley, 14th Earl of Derby	Conservative
1852–5	George Hamilton Gordon, Earl of Aberdeen	Conservative
1855–8	Henry John Temple, 3rd Viscount Palmerston	Whig
1858–9	Edward Smith Stanley, 14th Earl of Derby	Conservative
1859–65	Henry John Temple, 3rd Viscount Palmerston	Liberal
1865–6	Lord John Russell, 1st Earl Russell	Liberal
1866–8	Edward Smith Stanley, 14th Earl of Derby	Conservative
1868–8	Benjamin Disraeli	Conservative
1868–74	William Ewart Gladstone	Liberal
1874–80	Benjamin Disraeli (Earl of Beaconsfield from 1879)	Conservative
1880–5	William Ewart Gladstone	Liberal
1885–6	Robert Gascoyne-Cecil, 3rd Marquess of Salisbury	Conservative
1886–6	William Ewart Gladstone	Liberal
1886–92	Robert Gascoyne-Cecil, 3rd Marquess of Salisbury	Conservative
1892–4	William Ewart Gladstone	Liberal
1894–5	Archibald Primrose, 5th Earl of Rosebery	Liberal
1895–1902	Robert Gascoyne-Cecil, 3rd Marquess of Salisbury	Conservative

Significant Parliamentary Legislation during the Reign of Queen Victoria

1837   *Slave Compensation Act* (1 & 2 Vict. c. 3). Following the legislative abolition of the British slave trade in 1833 (3 & 4 Will. 4 c. 73), this act authorised the financial compensation of former slave owners in the Caribbean, Mauritius and Cape of Good Hope but afforded no reparations or material relief to the recently liberated populations.

1840   *Act to Extend the Practice of Vaccination* (3 & 4 Vict. c. 29). Enacted in a period in which smallpox posed a serious threat to public health, this legislation permitted Poor Law guardians to appoint medical officers to administer vaccination at public expense. The act also outlawed the common medical practice of variolation – the administration of infected matter from a sick individual to a healthy one as a prophylactic gesture.

1840   *Chimney Sweepers and Chimneys Regulation Act* (3 & 4 Vict. c. 85). The first of several acts which attempted to regulate the use of child labour in an industry in which the narrowness of chimney apertures and the presence of carcinogenic soot were everyday hazards for the so-called 'climbing boys'. The act prohibited individuals of both sexes under the age of twenty-one from climbing chimneys, though its provisions were frequently ignored by both employers and householders. Further legislation was necessarily enacted in 1864 (27 & 28 Vict. c. 37), 1875 (38 & 39 Vict. c. 70) and 1894 (57 & 58 Vict. c. 51).

1842   *Mines and Collieries Act* (5 & 6 Vict. c. 99). A further piece of legislation driven by an increasing awareness of the presence of child labour in the national economy, this act banned the underground employment of boys under the age of ten in the mining industry. Women and girls were, further, completely prohibited from working underground by the act, and individuals under fifteen were no longer allowed to operate machinery.

1844   *Factories Act* (7 & 8 Vict. c. 15). This act limited the daily working hours of women and all young persons under the age of eighteen to twelve hours on weekdays and nine on Saturdays: Sundays were culturally regarded as a day of spiritual contemplation, and this convention implicitly permitted physical rest also. Employees under the age of thirteen worked a maximum of six-and-a-half hours on weekdays and six on Saturdays, receiving in addition three hours of formal education on those days. The provisions of the act also specified the fitting of safety guards to dangerous machinery and prohibited children from cleaning beneath mill machinery while it remained in motion.

1845   *Slave Trade (Brazil) Act* (8 & 9 Vict. c. 122). Enacted in response to the continuing trade in slaves between Africa and Brazil, the act – popularly known as the 'Aberdeen Act', after its proposer, the Foreign Secretary Lord Aberdeen (1784–1860) – authorised the Royal Navy to apprehend and search any Brazilian ship suspected of being engaged in the slave trade, and rendered slave traders liable to be tried in British Admiralty courts.

1847   *Factories Act* (10 & 11 Vict. c. 29). Popularly known as 'The Ten Hour Act', this act enhanced the provisions of the 1844 legislation by imposing a maximum working day of ten hours, and a maximum working week of fifty-eight hours, for women and employees under the age of eighteen.

1848   *Public Health Act* (11 & 12 Vict. c. 63). An act which essentially enabled, rather than compelled, the intervention of local authorities in areas of sanitary concern. This legislation enabled existing borough corporations to take responsibility for the removal of refuse, for drainage, sewerage and water supplies, and for the paving of streets – these latter being in many places little more than repositories for refuse and the excrement of horses and other animals. A Central Board of Health was also established, though more substantial power was vested in the local boards established in areas where the death rate was higher than twenty-three per thousand.

1850   *Party Processions Act* (13 & 14 Vict. c. 2). Nominally an act 'to restrain party processions in Ireland', this legislation imposed restrictions on public processions, the display of flags and emblems, and the playing of music in Ireland following sectarian violence between Orangemen and Ribbonmen at Dolly's Brae (Magheramayo, County Down) in 1849. Though a number of prosecutions followed parades and gatherings organised by both sides of the religious and political divide, the marching traditions of both sides continued. The act was finally repealed in 1872.

1853   *Vaccination Act* (16 & 17 Vict. c. 100). The continued threat posed by smallpox provoked an extension of legislation passed in 1840, the 1853 act making vaccination compulsory for all children within three months of birth (or four months, if the child were in an orphanage). Parents who refused the vaccination – which was administered at public expense – could be fined. The compulsory administration of vaccination provoked resistance – sometimes violent – and also led to the foundation of an Anti-Vaccination League in 1853. The act was consolidated through further legislation in 1867 (30 & 31 Vict. c. 84) and by clarifications to the legal situation of those refusing vaccination in 1871 (34 & 35 Vict. c. 98) and 1874 (37 & 38 Vict. c. 75). A final act of 1898 (61 & 62 Vict. c. 49) permitted parents to refuse vaccination.

1857   *Matrimonial Causes Act* (20 & 21 Vict. c. 85). A significant reform of the law relating to marriage, which transferred divorce from ecclesiastical to civil law and effectively rendered conjugal relationship a contract rather than a sacrament. The act created a Court of Divorce and Matrimonial Causes, allowed legal separations to take place upon the grounds of adultery, cruelty or desertion, and permitted remarriage after divorce. Its provisions were biased in favour of the male complainant, who could petition for divorce on the grounds of adultery alone; his female counterpart, however, would be required to prove adultery aggravated by some additional element such as cruelty, incest or bigamy.

1857   *Obscene Publications Act* (20 & 21 Vict. c. 83). This act provided for the seizure and legal disposal of material deemed to be obscene – that is, calculated to corrupt the morals those who encountered it, or else offend the conventions of 'common decency'. A nominal attack on the commercial pornographers of London, the act failed to provide, however, an adequate definition of obscenity: this omission facilitated legal challenges to acts of seizure, most notably that of the case of *Regina* v. *Hicklin* (1868).

1858   *Medical Act* (21 & 22 Vict. c. 90). This legislation established a 'General Council of Medical Education and Registration' dominated by academically qualified clinicians through whose authority the qualifications of formally trained (rather than merely quack) practitioners might be verified. The provisions of the act further stated that only those regularly qualified in medicine or surgery might be employed as doctors within the Poor Law system.

1861   *Offences Against the Person Act* (24 & 25 Vict. c. 100). A compendious piece of legislation which covered murder, manslaughter and assault and the issuing of threats connected with these as well as consolidating the criminal implications of procuring abortions, bigamy, concealing the birth of a child and the manufacture of gunpowder to commit offences. The act maintained the illegality of sodomy, though substituting a term of hard labour for the earlier penalty of capital punishment, and set the age of sexual consent at thirteen years. The act did not apply in Scotland.

1864   *Contagious Diseases Act* (27 & 28 Vict. c. 85). The first of three separate pieces of legislation aimed at inhibiting the spread of venereal diseases, particularly among men serving in the armed forces, and of suppressing (or at least regulating) prostitution in seaports and garrison towns. The 1864 act permitted the police in certain specified garrison or port towns to apprehend any woman suspected of being engaged in prostitution in order to have her medically examined: any such woman found to be infected with syphilis or another transmissible complaint could then be confined in a lock hospital for up to three months. No provision was made under the act to either examine or restrict any man apprehended in the company of a prostitute or suspected of infection.

1866   *Contagious Diseases Act* (29 & 30 Vict. c. 35). An extension of the 1864 act which extended its jurisdiction to further naval ports, army towns and certain civilian areas. The emphasis of this second act would appear to be the suppression of perceived vice rather than a specific attempt to curb the spread of infection. The act increased the potential period of detention within the lock hospital system to twelve, rather than six, months but made no provision for the apprehension or restriction of the male clients of sex workers.

1867   *Factory Acts (Extension) Act* (30 & 31 Vict. c. 103). This legislation extended the provisions of the 1844 and 1847 *Factory Acts* – supplemented by related legislation specific to non-textile industries which had been passed in 1861, 1863 and 1864 – to all workplaces with over fifty employees. Further legislation in 1878, 1891 and 1895 regularised some aspects of the 1867 act by addressing potential loopholes in the employment of women and children in factories.

1867   *Representation of the People Act* (30 & 31 Vict. c. 102). The so-called 'Second Reform Act' substantially modified the terms of its predecessor of 1832 by granting a vote to all male householders in the urban boroughs as well as male lodgers who paid a rent of £10 or more annually. In the rural counties, the exclusion of women from the franchise was likewise maintained, though the property qualification for male voters was substantially reduced and comparatively small landowners and tenant farmers were enfranchised in consequence.

1868   *Pharmacy Act* (31 & 32 Vict. c. 121). This act associated a formal system of registration upon the qualification of pharmacists, and regulated the distribution of a named corpus of poisons through their businesses. These included strychnine and opium, restrictions placed upon the latter being unpopular due to the profitability of laudanum and patent medicines such as black drop.

1869   *Contagious Diseases Act* (32 & 33 Vict. c. 96). This final extension of the provisions of the similarly titled acts of 1864 and 1866 added further towns and cities to their jurisdiction, facilitated the detention of women who were not fit to be medically examined at the time of apprehension, and ostensibly provided for the moral and educational 'improvement' of individuals detained and medically treated for venereal disease. The provisions of all three *Contagious Diseases Acts* were repealed in 1886.

1869   *Irish Church Act* (32 & 33 Vict. c. 42). This legislation dissolved the historical union between the Anglican Church and the Church of Ireland. In so doing, it ended the collection of tithes by the Established Church and compensated those ministers deprived of this income, which was derived, in many cases, from a local population who followed a different faith. Under the act, the Irish Church no longer sent representative bishops to the House of Lords.

1870   *Elementary Education Act* (33 & 34 Vict. c. 75). Popularly known as 'Forster's Education Act', this was the first piece of parliamentary legislation which attempted to address working-class education on a national scale. The act retained the existing provision of local voluntary schools, many of them controlled by the Anglican Church, and supplemented these with locally funded and managed institutions which provided a non-denominational curriculum of religious studies as an accompaniment to basic numeracy and literacy. Elementary education in Scotland was similarly organised through the terms of the *Education (Scotland) Act* (35 & 36 Vict. c. 62).

1870   *Landlord and Tenant (Ireland) Act* (33 & 34 Vict. c. 46). This legislation attempted to correct a number of historical situations associated with tenant farming in Ireland at a time of increased land agitation. Its provisions applied the so-called 'Ulster Custom' of compensation for improvements across the island, and mandated compensation for those tenants evicted for causes other than non-payment of rent. The act also provided limited access to government loans for those tenants who were offered the opportunity to purchase their holding by a landlord.

1870   *Married Women's Property Act* (33 & 34 Vict. c. 93). An act which allowed married women to both inherit property and to retain control of any money which they earned in their own right through labour, investment or gift. Prior to 1870, these benefits would – except where some legal provision stated otherwise – automatically have become disposable at the will of the male spouse. The act was not retroactive and, as its title implied, did not apply to unmarried women – most notably to those under male guardianship through having not reached the legal age of majority.

1871   *Criminal Law Amendment Act* (34 & 35 Vict. c. 32). A Liberal measure which should be considered in the context of the 1871 *Trades Union Act*, this legislation imposed the possibility that severe penalties – including imprisonment with hard labour – could be applied to both pickets and to other union members who attempted to dissuade individuals from attending employment during industrial disputes, particularly through the application of coercive violence or the use of threats. It was repealed by the Conservative government in 1875.

1871   *Regulation of the Forces Act* (34 & 35 Vict. c. 86). One of the army reforms proposed by Edward Cardwell (1813–86), this act abolished the purchase of officer ranks in both the regular army and auxiliary forces, allocating compensation to those officers who had purchased a commission prior to its enactment. Promotion in the armed forces was, from this point, to be determined ostensibly by merit rather than patronage, social class or relative wealth.

1871   *Trades Union Act* (34 & 35 Vict. c. 31). Though the Royal Commission on Trades Unions, set up in 1867, was hostile to the decriminalising of trades union activity, some members of that body produced a minority report which influenced the eventual legislation. The act removed much of the legal restriction by which trades unions were deemed 'in restraint of trade' and thus inhibited the criminal prosecution of individual members. The *Criminal Law Amendment Act* which was passed by the Liberal government on the same day, however, placed certain restrictions on the physical actions that might be taken by trades unions and their members during an industrial dispute, thereby limiting much of the power granted by the *Trades Union Act*.

1871   *Universities Tests Act* (34 & 35 Vict. c. 26). This legislation built upon the precedents of the 1854 *Oxford University Act* (17 & 18 Vict. c. 81) and the 1856 *Cambridge University Act* (19 & 20 Vict. c. 88) by removing the remaining religious requirements (known as 'Tests') which prohibited Protestant dissenters, Roman Catholics, Jews and non-Christians, and those not professing any faith, from taking up professorships, fellowships, studentships or lay offices at the two oldest English universities. Prior to this act, senior academic positions and studentships might be awarded only to professing Anglicans.

1873   *Slave Trade Act* (36 & 37 Vict. c. 88). This act authorised the boarding and seizure, by the Admiralty or a representative of British colonial government, of any vessel suspected of being engaged in the slave trade.

1875   *Artisans' and Labourers' Dwellings Improvement Act* (38 & 39 Vict. c. 36). This act empowered local authorities to purchase and redevelop slum districts. Ironically, though the replacement housing was frequently more sanitary than the crowded accommodation it replaced, the rents charged were often in excess of the income available to the original inhabitants of the locality. In consequence, many slum dwellers simply moved to other low-cost areas, leading to additional pressure on existing slum locales. The provisions of the 1875 Act were extended by the 1885 *Housing of the Working Classes Act* (48 & 49 Vict. c. 72).

1875   *Conspiracy and Protection of Property Act* (38 & 39 Vict. c. 86). A Conservative measure which removed the provisions of the 1871 *Criminal Law Amendment Act*, thereby making picketing both legal and rendering the actions of pickets subject to the civil – rather than criminal – court system.

1876   *Elementary Education Act* (39 & 40 Vict. c. 79). Popularly known as 'Lord Sandon's Act', this legislation imposed upon parents a specific duty of care with regard to their children's education. School Attendance Committees were appointed in the interest of compelling attendance, and Poor Law guardians were empowered to assist families who were unable to afford school fees.

1876   *Royal Titles Act* (39 & 40 Vict. c. 10). This legislation permitted Queen Victoria to add the phrase 'Empress of India' to her existing title. The passing of the act was famously parodied on 15 April 1876 by John Tenniel (1820–1914) in *Punch* in the cartoon 'New Crowns for Old Ones'.

1880   *Elementary Education Act* (43 & 44 Vict. c. 23). Popularly known as Mundella's Education Act, this legislation imposed compulsory attendance at school for children aged between five and ten years, and imposed specific restrictions upon the employment of minors under the age of thirteen whose education might be considered to be deficient or incomplete.

1881   *Protection of Persons and Property (Ireland) Act* (44 & 45 Vict. c. 4). Popularly known as one of the 'Coercion Acts', this legislation facilitated the detention of individuals presumed 'under reasonable suspicion' to be involved in the organisation or implementation of agrarian disturbances, rent strikes, boycotting and other activities associated with the Home Rule campaign. Members of the Irish National land League were routinely detained under the act, which was repealed in 1894.

1882   *Married Women's Property Act* (45 & 46 Vict. c. 75). Covering England, Wales and Ireland (but not Scotland), this act defined the two partners in a marriage as discrete legal entities, formally permitting women to own, buy and sell property in their own right. The act further permitted women to both sue and be sued in their own right, with any damages awarded under the latter being the responsibility of the wife rather than of the husband. Similarly, one marital partner might be declared bankrupt independently of the other, ostensibly without detriment to the solvency of the latter.

1884   *Representation of the People Act* (48 & 49 Vict. c. 3). The so-called 'Third Reform Act' extended the voting qualifications applied in the urban boroughs to the rural counties, so that men who owned property valued at £10 or more, or who paid an annual rent of the same amount, were enfranchised. Women remained excluded from the franchise, though, and local variations in the value of land meant that fewer men were enfranchised by the act in Ireland than in England, Wales and Scotland.

1885   *Criminal Law Amendment Act* (48 & 49 Vict. c. 69). Specifically, 'An Act to make further provision for the Protection of Women and Girls, the suppression of brothels, and other purposes', this act raised the age of sexual consent from thirteen to sixteen, and set specific penalties for the rape (whether actual or attempted) and indecent assault of minors. The

Labouchère Amendment added a tariff of imprisonment not exceeding two years with hard labour to any man convicted of 'gross indecency' – effectively *any* ostensibly homosexual act other than sodomy – with another male, whether in public or in private.

1885   *Redistribution of Seats Act* (48 & 49 Vict. c. 23). Intimately related to the aspirations of the 1884 *Representation of the People Act*, this act attempted to structure representation upon a basis of equally populated parliamentary constituencies, with three separate boundary commissions advising on the redrafting of existing demarcations in England and Wales, Ireland and Scotland. Under the act, some existing seats were merged, others divided, and around 160 new seats were created, particularly in urban areas where parliamentary representation had not been adjusted to take account of recent population expansion.

1886   *Crofters Holding (Scotland) Act* (49 & 50 Vict. c. 29). Applicable only to Scotland, a piece of legislation with provisions related to rent and security of tenure of minor farmers (crofters) following a significant period of land agitation. The act appointed a Crofters' Commission to mediate on disputes between landlords and crofters, though it did little to reconfigure land ownership in Scotland, where large estates were rarely divided for sale to sitting tenants.

1886   *Shop Hours Regulation Act* (49 & 50 Vict. c. 55). This legislation restricted the working week for minors employed in shops to a maximum of seventy-two hours, inclusive of breaks for meals.

1889   *Official Secrets Act* (52 & 53 Vict. c. 52). This legislation created a series of offences based upon breach of official trust and the unauthorised disclosure of information, not merely by spies but also by individuals formally employed by the government or armed forces, or else subcontracted to work for these bodies. The legislation, which covered documents and plans as well as verbal information, reflected a growing uncertainty with regard to the relative position of the British in the context of perceived economic and military rivals at the close of the century.

1891   *Factory and Workshop Act* (54 & 55 Vict. c. 75). While many of the provisions of this legislation concerned matters related to the health and safety of the workforce, and transferred the responsibility or certain inspections to the oversight of local authorities, the act was notable for imposing a minimum age of eleven years for employees within factories.

1893   *Married Women's Property Act* (56 & 57 Vict. c. 63). This act amended the provisions of the 1882 Married Women's Property Act to the effect that married women were granted the same property rights as their single counterparts, and were thus enabled to enter into legal or financial contracts based upon the security of their own property.

1894   *Uniforms Act* (57 & 58 Vict. c. 45). This act prohibited the wearing of official military or naval uniforms by those not serving in the armed forces, an exception being provided for stage plays and similar situations where soldiers or sailors were being represented.

1896   *Locomotives on Highways Act* (59 & 60 Vict. c. 36). This act removed the earlier speed restrictions placed upon powered vehicles operating upon public highways, setting a speed limit of 14 mph (23 km/h) in most locations.

1897   *Weights and Measures (Metric System) Act* (60 & 61 Vict. c. 46). While not in any way substantially challenging the continued use of the imperial system of weights and measures, this legislation made the trade in goods sold in metric form legal, thus facilitating in particular commerce with European nations. Imperial measures remained the standard, however, for domestic trade and most commerce conducted within the British Empire.

1897   *Workmen's Compensation Act* (60 & 61 Vict. c. 37). Replacing the 1880 *Employer's Liability Act* (43 & 44 Vict. c. 42) – which merely empowered an injured employee to sue their employer for damages – this legislation made the owners of industrial premises liable to cover the medical costs of injuries sustained at work.

1900   *Mines (Prohibition of Child Labour Underground) Act* (63 & 64 Vict. c. 21). Child labour was still utilised in the British mining industry even following the 1842 *Mines and Collieries Act*. The 1900 act prohibited the employment underground of boys under the age of thirteen.

Figure 30 Obverse ('head') of 1895 penny showing profile of Queen Victoria and the royal titles in use at the end of the nineteenth century.

British Coinage

Formal name	Colloquial name and value in relation to other coinage
farthing	worth a quarter of a penny and written as ¼ d.
half penny	also known as a 'halfpenny' or 'ha'penny' and written as ½ d.
penny	the basic unit of small change, written as **1 d.**
threepence	colloquially 'thruppence' or the 'thruppeny bit' and written **3 d.**
groat	colloquially 'a joey' and worth **4 d.**
sixpence	worth half a shilling and written **6 d.**
shilling	colloquially 'a bob', worth twelve pennies and written **1/-**
florin	worth two shillings or **2/-**
half crown	worth two shillings and sixpence, written **2/6.**
crown	worth five shillings and written **5/-.**
half sovereign	worth ten shillings and written **10/-.**
sovereign	worth 20 shillings (one pound sterling) and written **£1 or L1**
Guinea	worth twenty-one shillings, and written **£1/1/-, 1 g.** or **1 gn**

The inscription on Victorian coinage varied across the years of the Queen's reign, though the formal titles of the monarch (given in Latin) were only to be found on the obverse side of the coin – colloquially the 'head', which featured a profile of the monarch. The 'tail' or reverse would customarily feature a symbolic figure, such as Britannia, and the designation of the coin's value. The monarchical titles, their abbreviations and main variations are as follows:

Abbreviation	Latin equivalent	English translation
DG *or* Dei Gra	Dei Gratia	By Grace of God
FD *or* Fid Def	Fidei Defensatrix	Defender of the Faith
Britt Reg	Brittanniarum Regina	Queen of the Britons
Reg	Regina	Queen
Ind Imp	Indiae Imperatrix	Empress of India (after 1877)

Imperial Weights and Measures

Distance				
Imperial	*Abbreviation*	*Imperial*	*Imperial*	*Metric*
1 inch	" or in	–	–	2.54 cm
1 foot	' or ft	12 inches	–	30.48 cm
1 yard	yd	3 feet	36 inches	91.44 cm
1 rod, pole or perch	rd	5½ yards	15 feet, 6 inches	5.029 m
1 chain	ch	4 rods	100 links	20.12 m
1 furlong	fur	220 yards	10 chains	201.17 m
1 mile	mi	320 rods	80 chains	1.609 km
Land mass or acreage				
1 acre	ac	4840 square yards		4047 m²
1 square mile	sq mi	640 acres		2.590 km²
Nautical measurement				
1 fathom	fth	2 yards	6 feet	1.829 m
1 nautical mile	nmi	1.151 miles 6080 feet		1.852 m
1 knot	kn	a velocity of 1 nmi per hour		1.852 km/h

Weight and mass (sometimes termed 'avoirdupois', or advp, measures)			
Imperial	*Abbrev*	*Imperial*	*Metric*
1 grain	gr	0.037 dr (0.002286 oz)	0.0648 g
1 dram	dr	27.344 gr (0.0625 oz)	1.772 g
1 ounce	oz	16 dr (437.5 gr)	28.35 g
1 pound	lb	16 oz (7,000 gr)	0.454 kg
1 stone	st	14 lb (224 oz)	6.35 kg
1 hundredweight	cwt	8 st (112 lb)	50.802 kg
1 ton	t	20 cwt (160 st)	1.06 tonnes

Note: The imperial hundredweight and imperial ton, as listed in the table above, may on occasion be referred to respectively as the 'long hundredweight' and 'long ton'; a 'short hundredweight' of 100 lb and a 'short ton' of 2000 lb are utilised in the United States. In addition to these commonly used weights, a system of troy measures (grain, pennyweight, ounce and pound) may also be encountered, specifically in the weighing of relatively small quantities of precious metals and jewels; and a system of apothecaries' measures (grain, scruple, dram, ounce and pound) is also employed in the manufacture of drugs and medicines.

Index

Note: Page numbers in *italics* refer to figures